HANOI
TODAY

VIRGINIA GIFT

HANOI TODAY

Images by an American Teacher in Vietnam

EBORY

Library of Congress Cataloging-in-Publication Data
Gift, Virginia
Hanoi Today: Images by an American Teacher/Virginia Gift

1. Vietnam - Description and travel
2. Vietnam - Description and travel - Views

Library of Congress Catalog Card Number 92-82953

ISBN 0-9633632-1-2

Published by

Ebory, Inc.
9635 Sea Shadow
Columbia, Maryland 21046
U.S.A.

Printed and bound in Italy

To my sons, Jonathan, Timothy and Christopher
— three classy, bright, interesting young men —
whose caring and whacky sense of humor
gets me through the bad days
and enriches the good ones.

Contents

Preface

The text in this book is about life in post-war Vietnam, but the photographs are all from the North, an area closed to the West from 1954 – the end of the French Indochina War – until 1987. The South had been open to Westerners up to unification of Vietnam in 1975, so photographs from that region are not rare, and although Saigon (Ho Chi Minh City) is interesting and beautiful, Hanoi is considered to be one of Asia's loveliest and best preserved cities. My goal was to capture its atmosphere before inevitable modernization occurs. More importantly, my hope is that these images convey some of the charm and spirit of the people who live in the North of Vietnam.

Acknowledgements

This book was made possible only with the help of many people. Being ashamed of my government's punitive post-war policies toward Vietnam, I went there as a volunteer, hoping to give something to a people I'd learned to admire through their history. But it didn't take long to realize I was receiving much more than I was giving.

I am beholden to my "official" Vietnamese students, as well as those where I consulted or visited regularly: The Institute for Foreign Affairs, the Hospital for Mothers and Newborn Children, the English department of The Amsterdam School, the translators and newscasters at the Voice of Vietnam radio station, the English department of Vietnam News Agency, the English Department at the University of Hanoi, and my favorite cyclo drivers at the Thang Nhat Hotel. Their curiosity, courage, dignity, perseverance, and sense of humor beguiled me; they represented humbling examples of a richness of spirit blooming in severe adversity.

I am deeply grateful to Paul Sonnenburg, my agent, editor, and good friend, who believed in this book before anyone else. His infectious enthusiasm and unfailing cheeriness frequently rescued me from total despair, and his efforts on my behalf have been truly Herculean— qualifying him for some sort of sainthood, somewhere.

I'm indebted to Judy and Dan Boyer, my publishers, who had the vision and compassion to want to bring to Western readers a softer, more realistic view of a country and people long isolated and demonized by the U.S.

Thanks are due to The American Friends Service Committee and The Christopher Reynolds Foundation who, after learning of my activities in Hanoi, offered grants to help cover some of my expenses. And I appreciate the administrators of The American School of Paris giving me two leaves of absence, though I suspect they were happy to have me so far away, in view of my propensity for telling them how to do their jobs.

My editor, Sidney Shore, spent months helping to shape the manuscript and sorting through the more than 3,000 slides. When Sidney retired, Leonard Porges inherited me; he's been extremely helpful, efficient, and supportive.

When I was in Hanoi, 1988-90, there was no American Embassy or other U.S. organization for back-up or support of any kind. Communication with the U.S. was almost nil, and I was cut off from friends, family, and my normal world. My morale was boosted by various American private aid workers who travelled regularly to Hanoi: Cherie Clarke, director of International Mission of Hope; Dr. Judy Ladinsky, Chair of the U.S. Committee for Scientific Cooperation with Vietnam; Don Luce of Asia Resource Center; Tom Vallely of the Harvard Institute for International Development.

They took film for processing, brought me news magazines, chocolates, and small necessities. I looked forward to their visits, not only for their good company, but because I admired them and learned much as they described their various hopes and projects for the people of Vietnam.

During my time in Vietnam, the government discouraged Vietnamese from having personal friendships with foreigners—outside official contacts. Thus, Hanoi's international community became a refuge and kept me from feeling too isolated. I was invited to join week-end sightseeing excursions, (invaluable to me, since there was no way to travel to out-of-the-way sites on my own, other than renting expensive government cars).

Swedish aid and embassy workers extended the hospitality of their homes, their swimming pool, and *t'ai chi* lessons; members of the French embassy included me on Sunday picnics at country pagodas—complete with the luxury of French cheeses, pates, and wine. The entire staff of the British Embassy, the ambassador on down, were especially kind to me. David Smith, head of the U.N. Development Program, helped solve problems with the Hanoi bureaucracy. Tore and Maureen Rose and Marylene Spezzati, also of the UNDP, were very helpful and became good friends.

I owe heartfelt thanks to an array of friends and acquaintances who read various drafts of the manuscript, or bolstered and encouraged me throughout my Vietnam-oriented projects. Tran Quoc Vuong, President of the Association of Hanoi Historians, took time from a busy schedule at a recent Cornell conference to give his opinions and suggestions on the manuscript, as did Steve Graw, Vietnamese scholar and bulwark of the Los Angeles - Vietnam Friendship and Aid Association. Phyllis Dreyfuss advised, edited, and sympathized as I struggled through my first book on the Vietnam War, parts of which are incorporated here. The librarians at the Wellfleet, Massachusetts library were cheerfully helpful. Barbara Roush, Barbara Kamm, Miranda Holt, Roy Gift, Renee and Bill Bowen, and Cleo Pollicott looked at drafts, listened to my agonizing, made suggestions, or have been supportive in one way or another.

A final note of personal thanks to family members. Mary Rabe, Tim Gift and Jonathan Gift cosetted me through computer crises; Chris Gift read the first draft, muttering "yuk" all the way through, but gave valuable suggestions on a much later draft.

Coming This Way: An Introduction

In 1979, as a history teacher at the American School of Paris, I was asked to create and teach a course on the Vietnam War, a request that changed my life. At first I refused. I'd spent the Vietnam War years in Paris teaching and raising three sons, and had not closely followed the war's events. But as I reflected on the matter that night, I decided I should know more about that chaotic period of United States history. The next day I agreed to develop the course and began to gather preliminary materials. Within days my initial interest caught fire and, fueled by the shock of discovery, swiftly grew into passion on its way to obsession.

When the new term began, I still had not located any single book that adequately covered this complicated war and its historic context. Finding the assignment of a hodge-podge of paperbacks and magazine articles too cumbersome for students, I finally decided to write my own textbook, a project that would consume five years, including a year's leave of absence from teaching.

The manuscript of my textbook was completed in 1987 just as Vietnam announced its re-opening to the West. Having immersed myself so long and so intently in Vietnam's story, I was seized with a consuming wish to visit the country just as soon as I could arrange to travel. But before I could turn my urgent wishes into reality, I needed a travel visa – no small task for an American in Paris acting as a private citizen and a Vietnamese Embassy staff for whom such a request was unprecedented. After months of visiting the embassy, I was directed to the French-Vietnamese Friendship Association, then organizing a three-week tour for a group of French physicians, health workers, and Indochina War veterans. I would join the group as its only non-French participant. Ill. 1-2

My travel companions fell in love with the Vietnamese (the veterans, all over again), and all of us were appalled by the misery we found across the land. We were impressed with the warmth of our welcome, the gentleness of the people, and the apparent absence of ill feeling toward us, coming as we did from countries that had tried for decades to conquer theirs. So impressed were we by their spirit that many of us talked of wanting to help them. Before the trip ended, a number of the doctors and medical personnel had arranged to return in some teaching or advisory capacity for short training sessions; a librarian offered to spend a year helping to organize library facilities neglected during the war. I too wanted to volunteer, but I could not then think of how I might meaningfully contribute to the vast needs of a developing and recovering nation.

During visits to hospitals and clinics, we learned of aid programs funded by private groups and nations worldwide, most of them modest, but at least making an effort to help. I keenly felt a personal shame and embarrassment about the current conduct of my own country toward the struggling Vietnamese. Since the end of the war, the United States had remained implacable. The American government did not merely refuse to assist in any way, but pursued policies that looked to many like little more than vengeance. Through a rigid trade and diplomatic embargo and overt hindrance of humanitarian aid projects and vetoes of aid from international financial organizations, every Administration since 1972 actively sought to keep Vietnam in a state of abject poverty. Ill. 3

In Hanoi I spoke with an Australian Embassy staff member responsible for selecting Vietnamese English teachers to go to Australia for language training. He told me that English was becoming Vietnam's second language, but that there was not one native English-speaking teacher in the country. Suddenly I knew how I could help: I determined on the spot to request a leave of absence from my position in Paris and to volunteer to teach English in Vietnam.

Doing good is not always as easy as it would seem. On my return to Paris, I contacted the Vietnamese embassy and told them of my idea. Once persuaded that I was serious, the staff there became enthusiastic. They said that while they could not pay a salary or transportation, the government could offer room and board. "Fine," I said, eager to be off. I soon learned that staff enthusiasm in Paris did not automatically generate action in Hanoi, where no one seemed overwhelmed at the prospect of me showing up with chalk and good intentions. I sent numerous letters and telexes to the Ministry of Education. Silence from Hanoi. For more than nine months I dispatched copies of my dossier – some hand-carried by aid workers, some delivered to Vietnamese officials visiting Paris, some by ordinary mail. Still silence. Phone calls to American aid organizations operating projects in Vietnam proved discouraging. Indochina hands told me there was no way Hanoi would give a resident visa to an American, and recited stories of rejected applications for their own English-language volunteers.

June arrived; I'd taken a leave from my job, sublet my apartment, and would have to make other plans if I couldn't go to Vietnam. Among my students was a young woman whose father was then Sweden's ambassador to the Organization for Economic Cooperation and Development (OECD) and who had been ambassador to Hanoi in the late 1970s. At my urgent request, the diplomat kindly contacted his embassy in Hanoi. Within a week he'd received a telex for me: I was welcome to teach in Hanoi, but there were no funds available to pay for my living expenses. In spite of the additional expense, I was determined to proceed.

Three months later and two hours out of Bangkok, my plane was descending toward Hanoi Airport. I looked down at a landscape scarred by flooded bomb craters scattered as far as the eye could see. I recalled with wonder the series of events that had led a past-middle-age woman to be the first American since the war to come to live independently in Vietnam, perhaps the only one ever in North Vietnam.

I'd dismissed the admonitions of friends and family members who felt I was taking a foolish risk in going to a country where there was no protection of an American embassy, where an American could expect to be despised, and where vengeance could be taken by individuals or by a hostile and often capricious government. While I had no fear for my personal safety, I was a bit concerned about what my life would be like in the coming months. Minor details suddenly seemed important. What if no one met me at the airport? I knew there were no taxis or buses at the airport, thirty miles from Hanoi. (Foreign travelers were not permitted into Vietnam without an official sponsor who was obligated to meet their planes.) No public telephones or phone books existed, nor did I know the number of the person at the Institute where I was assigned to teach. I didn't know where I would be living. How would I ask for help? The few words of Vietnamese I'd learned from expatriates in Southern California would not take me far.

Less urgent problems lingered in my mind. What sort of classes would I be teaching? Who would my students be? How many hours would I be working? Would there be chalk? (Yes, but it crumbled when I wrote fast.) Would I have books to teach from? (No.) How risky was carrying my money in cash (credit cards and travelers' checks could not be used)? How would I keep in touch with my stateside family when mail delivery required three to six months or forever, and the telephone was ruled out by an antique system and a U.S. embargo on calls to Vietnam? What would happen if I got sick or hurt in this land where health care delivery was problematic for everyone?

As the Thai Airways plane taxied toward the terminal, I saw only one other plane on the tarmac, an airliner of Aeroflot, the Soviet airline. Water buffalo grazed alongside the narrow runway next to peasants in conical bamboo hats, who were gathering some sort of greens. Two small hangars stood nearby, one of them missing part of its roof. Inside the one-story terminal building – little more than a large shed – were three small rooms. My fellow passengers – Vietnamese and a few Western embassy employees or technicians on temporary assignment – went into the first one. A layer of dust covered everything. Dull ocher paint flaked off bare walls and woodwork. We lined up in front of four wooden sentry boxes, where customs officials minutely scrutinized each passport, smiled, then pulled back a wooden bar admitting the traveller into the next area. Passengers filled out two long and complicated sets of forms, twice – no carbon paper. In my nervous fiddling with papers, passport, and money, I dropped my eyeglasses, which shattered. I'd brought two extra pairs with me, but wondered how long they'd last at this rate.

Ill. 4

As the last customs official stamped my documents, a young man stepped forward and introduced himself: Le Hong Lam, from the Foreign Ministry. Replying to his stilted but understandable English, I offered my much-rehearsed greeting in Vietnamese, which seemed to puzzle him. However, he made me feel welcome by saying, "We've all been waiting for you since June." Once I'd settled into the car behind the driver, Lam delivered a few obviously prepared words about my coming to live in Vietnam. "You are the first brick in building relations between our two countries," he said, in a phrase I would hear repeated by officials and individual citizens throughout my stay.

Knowing that housing was scarce in the diplomatic enclaves and that foreigners were not permitted to live on their own, I had anticipated living in one of the downtown hotels set aside for persons awaiting accommodation in the foreigners' apartment compounds. Instead, on the edge of town we pulled up to a scruffy-looking hotel, a typical example of concrete-slab socialist realism that seemed near collapse. The entry-way looked dirty (I'd not yet learned about Hanoi dust) and none of the day's bright sunshine penetrated into the dark, cold lobby. The hotel had been chosen for me, Lam said, because it was close to the Institute of Foreign Affairs where I would be teaching. My dismay was relieved a bit when the two women behind the desk greeted me with sweet, enthusiastic smiles and said they were honored to have an American in their hotel. Their English was halting, but clear – superior, I would soon discover, to that of the staff at any of the more popular hotels for foreigners. The $22-a-day rate seemed high, but I learned that other hotels charged from $35 to $45, much overpriced for their quality. As in other Communist countries at the time, foreigners paid a higher rate than local people. Lam left me to get settled in, promising to pick me up the next morning.

Ill. 5

My dingy room was barely large enough to hold a single bed with threadbare sheets, a small wardrobe with no hangers, a miniature dresser with two tiny drawers, a stuffed plastic chair with no arms, and hardly room enough to stretch out my legs when I sat down. But I was delighted to see a small refrigerator and air-conditioner, both essential for Westerners coping with Hanoi's soaring summer heat and humidity. The walls were unadorned institutional beige. A bare bulb hung by its wires from the ceiling. The bathroom was perhaps four feet square, with pitted gray concrete walls and floor. The broken toilet seat required ingenuity for effective use. The shower's hot water tap handle turned the entire tap; and, unhindered by any sort of stall, the showerhead jutting from the wall sprayed water all over the dirty-looking floor. Hot water was only sporadically available; I never did figure out the schedule, if there was one. Over a rusted sink hung a mirror with much of its silver backing peeled off; below, a plastic bucket. Depressing. My discovery of the rats and the ants was yet to come. I wandered back into the bedroom and lovingly fingered the two beautifully embroidered, sparkling white pillow slips, the only items not solely utilitarian.

After lunch I decided to get out of the dreary hotel, but outdoors was little improvement in this neighborhood wholly devoid of the charm of downtown Hanoi. All around loomed the worst sort of socialist, egg-carton concrete apartment blocks, with make-shift lean-tos patched onto terraces, laundry flapping from windows, and no leaf of green in sight. I wanted to go downtown to shop for some things to make my room more comfortable and cheerful. At the hotel desk I asked about the going rate for a ride into town on a cyclo (Hanoi's three-wheeled, collapsible-hooded pedicab, with the driver in back). The clerks found it amusing that I wanted to take a cyclo, and I later learned that foreigners are always chauffeured about in government automobiles. Undaunted, I scoured the streets until I found a cyclo driver and negotiated a price, using the Vietnamese custom of dealing with foreigners by writing numbers on the palm of my hand with a ballpoint pen.

Ill. 6

My few words of Vietnamese seemed merely to puzzle my willing driver. After listening patiently for several minutes, he finally said what I interpreted to mean "Diplomatic Intershop?" I said OK, figuring correctly that our compromise destination would at least get me downtown. There I bought an armful of baskets, a small handwoven rug, some pottery, and a Russian electric kettle for boiling my drinking water. After taking my parcels back to the hotel, I went out and bought a bicycle. Then I tried to find again the tiny shop where I'd changed money on the black market during my visit the year before. I worried about changing money illegally and pictured myself in a dank cell, a forlorn and isolated capitalist. But I knew that I couldn't possibly afford the luxury of the legal exchange rate of 700-900 dong to the dollar, compared to the black market rate of 3,500.

Early next morning, Lam and a driver picked me up to go to the Institute for a meeting with my new colleagues. During the meeting to discuss the details of what I would teach to the Foreign Ministry employees, I was pleasantly surprised when the administrators agreed to my suggestion that – since there were no text books – I teach my specialty of American history and politics. I had brought a large selection of news clippings from home and put them on the table, suggesting a review to determine which would be most appropriate – a diplomatic way, I felt, to give my hosts an opportunity to veto the articles. The materials were gently slid back to me with the reply, "Use anything you wish."

As we returned to my hotel, Lam told me that he had been appointed my "guardian angel" for the time I would be in Vietnam. He was to be my interpreter and guide, available at all times; he'd been relieved of his regular duties for the length of my stay. My reactions were mixed. The attention was flattering but, lost as I might feel, I had no intention of being baby-sat. Adventurers don't have their hands held!

Classes were to begin the following day, so I asked Lam to come on his bicycle to show me the way to the Institute. Thereafter, I said, I'd get there on my own bicycle. Morning brought a raging monsoon storm. I donned my hooded plastic poncho and we set off together. There were so many bicycles and so many holes in the dirt roads that traffic could only inch along. Cyclists gingerly skirted round the larger puddles while the four-wheeled vehicles drove straight down the middle, flinging sheets of muddy water over cyclists and pedestrians. After more than half an hour, we arrived; I was drenched and muddy head to toe. Lam pointed to the fourth-story balcony of the building directly in front of us and said my class had come early to greet me. Smiles and waves encouraged me as I squished up the four flights of stairs, embarrassed about my bedraggled appearance. (Later I was amused to discover that the students had upbraided Lam because he hadn't arranged for the Institute's car and driver to pick me up. It wasn't fitting, they said, for a foreign teacher to ride a bicycle. After I moved into the center of town, the Institute did provide me with a car and driver to and from class.)

Ill. 7

By the time I reached the fourth floor, the students were all standing by their desks, smiling wonderful smiles. On the teacher's desk stood a glass of fresh-squeezed fruit juice and a pot of tea (no mere gesture, the fresh libations would grace my desk each teaching day). One of the students (every class or group in Vietnam has a class "spokesman" or leader) gave a moving, obviously painstakingly prepared speech of welcome, and presented me with a bouquet of pink roses from someone's garden. Before many minutes of the first class had passed, I realized that my students, employees of the Foreign Ministry and ranging in age from twenty-three to fifty-nine, were a teacher's dream. Their excitement at meeting their first American,

1 Huge crowds throng to see girls dance in traditional costumes at the Dong Da Festival.

2 Heading home from the rice fields at dusk, a group of peasants heads across a dike with their water buffalo and tools.

3 Icy winter weather scarcely slows a peasant woman gathering firewood and edible greens in the North.

4 Unprepossessing Hanoi Airport, its hangars dilapidated, its service buildings far below world standards, awaits development.

5 Among the buildings best known to diplomatic visitors, Vietnam's Foreign Ministry Reception Building is the former residence of the French High Commissioner for Tonkin (North Vietnam). The author resided for much of her time in Hanoi in the Foreign Ministry Guest House Hotel, just behind this building.

6 With little prospect of replacement anytime soon, every machine is constantly maintained and repaired, often by resourceful operators like this cyclo driver.

7 Downtown Hanoi traffic presents a ceaseless kaleidoscope of old and new, an endless flow of contrasts.

8 Clattering slowly along after many decades, a few dilapidated streetcars still serve some pre-French parts of Hanoi.

9 Permitting their users to carry loads of great weight and awkward shape, bamboo shoulder poles remain a principal transport device.

10 Like many bridges heavily damaged during the war, this one in the North is kept serviceable with planks, wire, and nails.

8

9

10

11 Running on the country's narrow gauge railway, 1920-era steam locomotives haul daily passenger and freight trains between Hanoi and Ho Chi Minh City.

12 Wherever there are rivers and canals, small boats take the place of cyclos and bicycles for moving goods to and from markets, and act as water taxis, too.

13 Because many bombed-out bridges remain to be rebuilt, ferry-boats flourish—like this one which carried a party of Swedish diplomats and the author on an excursion into the countryside.

11

12

14 After an hour-long rowboat ride from Hanoi, and a strenuous climb, the devoted pilgrim is rewarded with this view of an elaborately wrought pagoda.

13

14

15 Shielded from the bright midday sun, a young woman pauses to rest from work digging clay in a field near Hanoi.

16 Among the instruments popular at festivals, drums rank high, and this young drummer takes his role at a Buddhist festival most seriously.

17 Intent on the celebration of a Buddhist festival, this man and woman wear traditional headgear; he a pleated cap, she a black velvet turban.

15

16

18 At festival time, the array of traditional costumes exhibits dazzling variety in form, color, and texture; this cap incorporates figures worked in glass beads.

19 Poised and serene, the face of this Vietnamese monk seems to exemplify the calm determination displayed by so many of his countrymen.

18

19

their thirst for any knowledge I could share with them, made the teaching experience unlike any other I'd ever had. Suddenly my misgivings and disappointments vanished. Before retiring that evening, I began plotting ways to extend my stay in Hanoi past the four-month visa period. I eventually spent the greater part of two academic years in the city.

Living in Vietnam

Living in Vietnam was a schizophrenic experience. On the one hand, I felt privileged to be living an adventure, waking each day knowing that I was going to learn something new, meet interesting people, do things I couldn't do back home. Work was a joy; I'd never felt more appreciated as a teacher. (Where else can a teacher be assured of thank-yous and huge smiles when she offers to extend class time by half an hour?) Word of my presence soon spread and I was besieged with requests to teach English. I ended up spreading myself too thin: I gave classes for hospital doctors and administrators, to Vietnamese public school English teachers, and at the English division of the state-run radio; I consulted at the Vietnamese News Agency, the country's wire service; and even coached some of the cyclo drivers who hung out by the Thang Nhat hotel.

I was on my bicycle every day, photographing and exploring, stopping at tiny pagodas, making mental notes of passageways that looked intriguing for future exploration. Early on I decided to take as many photographs as I could because, as I learned about proposed high rise hotels and other "benefits" of Westernization, I became certain that Hanoi would soon begin to lose its charm, and I wanted to record the city as it was. Hanoi, like Paris, is a visual feast, and I never tired of exploring it.

On the other hand, the destitution in which most Vietnamese live is devastating – conditions simply unimaginable in the West. Too vivid still in my mind are scenes such as an old woman sitting on the curbstone eating rotten banana peels from a refuse pile. Sometimes I would follow an old woman in tatters for several blocks, until there was a place where I could slip a bit of money to her without attracting attention. (When I was in Vietnam, per capita income there hovered below that of Bangladesh.) I didn't recall having been so disturbed by the poverty on my previous visit, and I conjectured that perhaps poverty is easier to look at if you know you'll soon be leaving it.

However, compared to other poor countries where despair, sullenness, and apathy are apparent and pervasive, people in Vietnam's streets are busy and smiling; most express the belief that things will soon get better.

Hanoi can be exceedingly frustrating for a Westerner. Because of the triple-canopied bureaucracy and the paranoia bred through long years of totalitarianism, accomplishing even the smallest task takes on mammoth proportions. Nothing works, and almost nothing Westerners take for granted is available. Living without English-language newspapers, news magazines, and books doesn't seem reasonable after a while. Boiling my drinking water every morning soon lacked quaintness, and riding a bicycle lost its charm on cold, rainy days . . . as did needing to have my bicycle tires repaired every few days, dirty toilets, dust everywhere, and . . . no cheese. The lack of a viable telephone system necessitated many trips to an office to arrange an appointment, which might be canceled, requiring still more trips, ad infinitum.   Ill. 8-10

You didn't decide at the last moment you'd like to take a weekend excursion or picnic in the country, since permission had to be obtained from the police each time you left the city – local residents and foreigners alike. I was never refused permission, but I always resented the hassle of having to get the papers. Later I would learn that I'd unwittingly bent and broken all sorts of rules and conventions. Disapproving officials hadn't known quite what to do with this unprecedentedly unclassified alien, but since my visa ran for a mere four months they apparently left me alone in the belief that I'd be gone soon enough.

In part because I believed that Westerners' movements were officially monitored, and partly because Hanoi is really a small town in spite of its nearly three million citizens, I often felt as if I were living in a goldfish bowl. If I visited an office in the morning, by noon someone across town would ask me why I had been there. Other Westerners told of similar experiences.

Moreover, the fact of Hanoi's isolation was never far out of mind. The city's one interurban train – to Saigon – was off-limits to non-Vietnamese. But since a prospective passenger in moderately good health could run about as fast as the locomotive could travel, the train wasn't considered a valid means of transportation anyway. Likewise, boats out of Haiphong were denied to foreigners. There remained only the airplanes departing for Bangkok several times each week. Occasionally embassy and UN diplomatic mail pouches didn't arrive for weeks, an aggravatingly routine source of grumbling among the city's non-resident community. Especially dispiriting was the absence of telephone contact with family and friends. Trying to sort out a garbled message about one of my sons from an intermediary in Bangkok one afternoon, I frustratedly told British embassy friends that I felt like getting on the plane to
Ill. 11 Bangkok just to make a phone call. "We know people who have done just that," they said.

This isolation, combined with the frustrations of daily living, induced a sort of cabin fever which led most Westerners to escape as often as possible to posh Bangkok. There they could shop for clothing and food (some embassies forbade staff to buy any food in Vietnam), have their hair cut, make long distance phone calls, and enjoy other recreation. Much talk at Hanoi dinners or receptions was the next trip to "The World." Because of the expense, I had no such option, and Western colleagues wondered aloud about how I could remain in Hanoi for so long without a break. Some thought me a bit strange. Not a few times, I felt sorry for myself because I couldn't go off to "the outer world" of Bangkok.

But such lapses made little sense, because I loved living in Hanoi, and so did just about every other Westerner I knew. Many renewed their contracts more than once in order to stay on. When someone learned that an application for extension had been denied, we all commiserated. With rare exceptions, Westerners liked and admired the Vietnamese people – though few had any kind words for the government – and all were passionate in their affection for Hanoi.

Because of the U.S. government's continued hostility to their country, and because there had obviously been hesitation before Hanoi took up my offer to work as a volunteer, I had fully expected to be under suspicion by Vietnamese officialdom. Soon after arriving, I heard rumors of questions being asked. "What is she really doing here?" "Why is she taking so many pictures of embassies?" (Answer: embassies are housed in wonderful French colonial villas.) One ambassador from a Middle Eastern nation advised a Belgian woman working for the United Nations not to associate with me because I was an "American spy." Nor was I surprised when Vietnamese friends told me of some official suspicion of me. I was not prepared, however, to be suspect among the Western community.

Before long, I discovered that more than a few people in the foreign diplomatic community (all Europe is represented) believed I was in Hanoi as a "deep cover" operative of the Central Intelligence Agency. Because Vietnamese were not then permitted to spend social time alone with foreigners (a rule not always honored), I was compelled to make friends among Westerners and was disappointed that no one seemed particularly delighted to have me around. The Swedish ambassador graciously asked his First Secretary to include me in some of the embassy social functions. Later, several women in the British embassy took pity on me and began to include me in dinner parties and – more important to me – sightseeing excursions to the countryside. (Because I lacked the funds to hire government cars, and because public transport is totally unreliable, I was completely dependent on the international community for travel outside Hanoi.) The British ambassador, when I told him I was unable to receive mail, kindly offered to let me use his diplomatic pouch. He also added my name to the embassy evacuation list, which helped me to feel a bit less isolated. Eventually, through the British and

Swedes, I became a part of the international community and met numerous lovely and interesting people, many of whom remain my friends.

Ill. 12-14

But my spy rep never entirely died. At dinners, when conversation turned to embassy gossip, someone invariably said, "Virginia, turn off the recorder." Visiting technical experts would ask if I worked for the CIA; I routinely replied that I would be delighted to earn big money working as a spy, but nobody had yet asked me. On the morning of my departure from Hanoi, Stan Reedy, the Mennonite Central Committee representative from Bangkok, told me of a conversation in the Thai capital during which my name came up. Someone had immediately said, "Oh, she's that American spy." Dr. Reedy, in some annoyance, asked the fellow if he'd ever met me; no, the man said, he'd only heard about me. I found the whole phenomenon amusing, partly because I suspected that my government was something less than euphoric about my being in Hanoi at all, let alone likely to hire me to gather information. Besides, I never determined what sort of information I might have gathered that would interest anyone in the government.

I soon came to accept that most Vietnamese I met spoke to me as though I was privy to U.S. government plans and thoughts, and I was often asked when my country was going to normalize diplomatic relations with Hanoi. But I was more perplexed at being treated much the same way by many Europeans. At social events I was often admonished about something Washington had recently done, and when the Vietnamese pulled their troops out of Cambodia, everyone felt the United States would honor its commitment to recognize Vietnam "once the troops went home." I spent a few uncomfortable weeks when it became clear that Washington had changed the rules; people expected me to explain, and I obviously could not.

The only anti-American attitudes I encountered came from the international community. An American aid worker who visited Vietnam monthly told of sitting next to an Australian embassy employee on the Bangkok-Hanoi plane. When she'd identified herself as an American, she reported, the Australian coldly informed her that no one wanted the Americans to come to Hanoi because "they would try to run everything, and bring their cultural devastation with them – in the form of Coca Cola signs and fast food restaurants." No one said so to my face, but it didn't take me long to conclude that many people wanted to keep Hanoi to themselves.

Some people who did not believe I was a CIA agent presumed that I was a Communist, or a Communist sympathizer. Why else would I come with offers of help? The first person to ask if I were a Communist was a visiting journalist from a Japanese Communist newspaper. I was taken aback. After all, in the States no one would presume to ask such a question, since no one in America would be expected to admit it. But I just laughed, and said that I was much too much of a hedonist to be a Communist – another of my stock replies.

Conversely, the idea of the capitalist as ordinary person was alien to a generation of Vietnamese raised on propaganda that excoriated the evils of capitalist society and denounced its members as running-dog-imperialist pigs, and other not so gentle things. One day I'd asked my Ministry class to prepare oral reports on any books or short stories they'd recently read. A young man stood up and told of an American Western story in which a "poor farmer boy was in love with the daughter of a neighboring capitalist rancher." I interrupted him to say that the term "capitalist" was not necessary, since everyone in America is a capitalist. (Not precisely true, but close enough.) The concept of an entire country filled with capitalists was not something my students were ready to handle, and their minds were obviously boggled at the thought of so many of these rare creatures in one place. The emotions that registered on their faces ranged from horror to incredulity, and finally – when they saw my amused response to their reactions – we all had a long, wonderful laugh.

Meeting the People

The Americans I've spoken with about my experiences in Vietnam ask, "What are the Vietnamese really like?" While generalities drawn from one observer's personal experience, no matter how rich and varied, can be only a fragment of truth, I offer my own observations, impressions, and anecdotes of the Vietnamese people today as one woman's carefully considered reflection of a profoundly moving experience.

Immediately evident among the Vietnamese is their candid willingness to laugh at themselves, and their inclination to find humor in any situation. I don't mean just smiles, I mean rollicking belly-laughs, head thrown back, eyes sparkling. A not infrequent topic of conversation among the international community was the question of how people living in dire, post-war poverty could retain any richness of spirit at all, let alone this cheery irrepressibility. A word often chosen by foreign observers to characterize the Vietnamese is "indomitable."

The people seem to harbor no bitterness about either their present plight or about the suffering endured in the wars. They seem nonplussed by America's apparent obsession with the war and, most importantly, the U.S. refusal to recognize Vietnam diplomatically. One official told me, "The French don't hold a grudge, even though they lost much more than the Americans in their war." No Vietnamese I met introduced the subject into conversation, nor did they avoid the topic if it arose. Most seemed to dismiss the war as just one more bad patch in their history. They want to get on, to continue to improve their lives.

The rich Vietnamese spirit is also evident in their generous hospitality and warm welcome. Every visitor to Vietnam leaves with a suitcase crammed with souvenirs for his family, formally presented by officials or people with whom they've spent a bit of time. Nothing is expected in return. One day, when I'd arranged for the Institute to lend me a car and driver, translator Lam and I visited a traditional pottery-making village near Hanoi. There I was taken around to see the communal workshops and visited the homes of the most important potters. At each small house I was offered tea, iced coffee (a luxury there which I detest, but which I dutifully sipped), fruit, cakes, and a selection of beautiful ceramic pots, mugs, bowls, and sculptures. I soon had more than I could carry, and two large cartons were produced from somewhere so that Lam and my driver might bear the treasures to the car.

To observe the pleasure taken by the Vietnamese in sharing what little they have with strangers is a humbling experience. In the city or countryside, if you stop to greet someone outside their home, you are immediately offered a cup of tea. If you accept and sit at their sidewalk table or go inside their home, more likely than not small cakes and fruit will appear out of nowhere while tea is being prepared. One group of touring American high school students told me of a Vietnamese teenager who insisted on giving one of them the shirt off his back, as a souvenir, and he would accept nothing in return. The young American was near tears as she told me, "Here are people who have almost nothing, yet they are willing to share with strangers. This trip has changed my life."

Ill. 15-22

The legendary Vietnamese politeness must be experienced to be appreciated, and visitors from abroad sometimes find the climate of personal respect and dignity in Hanoi a startling contrast. Two young British tourists who had just arrived in Hanoi after several months in China, where loud talking, pushing, shoving, and invading personal space are apparently common, told me of their astonishment at how Vietnamese treated them and one another – no jostling for a place in a line for theater tickets or a seat on the bus, or for paying a cashier in a crowded store. Tempers stay cool even in the city's bizarrely chaotic traffic.

Subtle courtesy prevails in more complex interactions as well. Although almost everyone exhibits enthusiastic curiosity about a stranger's family and home country, few would dream of satisfying that curiosity if they felt they were intruding. Tourists, still rare and an object of interest, are seldom bothered on the streets of Hanoi, although this is not always the case in

Saigon. Even though someone in public may overhear you talking and be simply bursting to experiment with a few phrases of English, your privacy is respected; only if you look as though you would welcome conversation are you approached.

The Vietnamese touch one another in public rather more than is common in the West. Although public demonstrations of affection of a sexual nature between men and women are not usual, people are unembarrassed by friendly touching among persons of the same sex. Talkers touch one another's shoulders or arms when making conversational points, and members of the same sex stroll the streets arm-in-arm or hand-in-hand. While sitting through a long meeting or entertainment, I've seen middle-aged men or women openly place a hand on a friend's knee, and let it rest there. In social situations and business meetings, everyone sits close to each other, even when there is plenty of room. At first I was a bit put off by this intrusion into my personal space, especially when first meeting people, but I soon learned to adapt.

Vietnamese of both sexes are soft-spoken and discreet, and are frequently described by outsiders as "sweet" or "soft." At first I thought this labeling might have been simply my own, feminine, vocabulary, but I have often heard foreign men choose the same terms to characterize the Vietnamese personality. Exceptions to this behavior pattern are rare. Outsiders also consider the Vietnamese gentle, and "not the least hostile." How to reconcile such seeming mildness with the irrefutable evidence that these men and women rank among the world's toughest warriors? Having lived and traveled extensively in countries where machismo prevails, my guess is that here is a people, a national community, whose experience has shown them that not even the most formidable alien powers can destroy them or crush their spirit. With their history, there must have developed an enduring confidence that needs no macho facade.

A visitor with only the briefest experience of walking about the streets of Hanoi will not be surprised to learn that the Vietnamese are esteemed among the most disciplined and hardest-working labor force in Southeast Asia. Is this, too, a result of their thousands of years of having to work so hard for independence?

Ill. 23-25

Although I was aware of the historic fact, the results of the isolation in which northern Vietnamese have lived since 1954 frequently brought me up short. I was often startled as I spoke with educated, literate Hanoians who knew nothing whatsoever about the most ordinary aspects of life in the West. It seemed I was forever explaining how the American government works. One of the reasons why so many Vietnamese felt I was an American government spy was because they couldn't imagine a country where people were free to travel to countries – like theirs – with whom the government maintained no relations. Repeatedly I was questioned about how long it took to get permission to come to Vietnam. The notion of a free press seemed beyond their comprehension. And my new friends were further perplexed by a government whose branches argued among themselves in public.

But it wasn't simply the mysterious intricacies of government abroad that intrigued them. The details and patterns of ordinary daily Western life proved endlessly intriguing as they read the news articles I'd brought from the United States and pondered my explanations. Checking accounts, credit cards, shopping malls, Disneyland, personal computers, heavy metal music, junk food ("How can food be junk?"), sitcoms, cops-and-robbers movies, drive-in banks and restaurants, Marilyn Monroe – all were unheard of. The quirky metaphors of English, as they do for anyone not born to them, sometimes complicated the process of discovery. In a country that cooks on charcoal braziers or single electric rings, it took careful exposition – and several drawings – to elucidate the phrase, "it was put on the back burner."

On one occasion, soon after restrictions on private enterprise were loosened, several Vietnamese were marvelling at what a change the impromptu street markets made in Hanoi's atmosphere. One said, as the other nodded in agreement, "Now it's just like Bangkok," although neither commentator was likely to have ever been to the dazzling Thai capital, or even to have seen photographs of it. I found their pride and confidence in their country's progress very touching.

Although not everyone would travel out of Vietnam if given the opportunity, everyone thirsts for knowledge of life outside their country's borders. Even though I always mentioned to new acquaintances that I live in Paris, no one wanted to hear about that wonderful city. They only had ears for the United States, and pleaded for details of life in America – courtship, marriage, housing, labor-saving devices in the home, child rearing, education, and entertainment. I didn't get the impression they wanted to move to America, but they wanted to bring the American version of what they consider to be the "good life" to Vietnam.

The apparent American preoccupation with acquisition of "things" perplexed my students. I once tried to explain shopping malls as a source of entertainment in America. This concept was bewildering; if the Vietnamese need something, they arrange to make it themselves, or have it made by friends. Only as a last resort is something purchased. The idea that anyone would consider it a valid form of entertainment to walk around shops searching for something to spend money on was a notion that might have originated on Mars.

Many Vietnamese misconceptions about the United States were negative, originating in a previously hostile Soviet and Eastern bloc press. I don't know how many people asked me with great concern about how Vietnam could help America's "lonely old people," those abandoned aged thrust out of their families to live in slum-type institutions or eking out survival alone in dingy rooms, eating dog food. Many in Hanoi are appalled at America's problems with drugs and crime and racism, which they believe to be even worse than the admittedly grim reality. Many found it difficult to believe when I told them that blacks have been elected to positions of power in several large cities. Clearly, in the past their government neglected to report positive news about America, just as American administrations and media have shown little interest in promulgating positive information about Vietnam.

Since 1973 and until very recently, Americans have heard little about the Vietnamese, their history, or their civilization. One purpose of this book is to shine a bit of light on a land and its people whom Americans – some for very painful reasons – have tried to forget. It would be productive indeed if Americans could become as interested in Vietnam as the Vietnamese are in the United States.

Modern Hanoi

"Whether it is blossom time or not,
Jasmine is always jasmine.
Elegant or not,
One is nevertheless a citizen of the capital."

Nguyen Cong Trung, Nineteenth century

The Face of Hanoi

To visit Hanoi is to enter a time warp, an anomaly of old world charm in the capital city of one of Southeast Asia's largest nations. I met French Indochina War veterans who simply could not believe their eyes when they saw that the center of Hanoi was exactly the way it had been when they left. Said one, "What other capital city in the world has remained unchanged in over thirty years?"

Because the city generates no industrial air pollution, a sky full of stars glimmers each cloudless night. Traffic is chiefly bicycles, cyclos, animal-drawn carts, and porters struggling under heavily-laden bamboo shoulder-poles. Exhaust fumes from the few motor vehicles have not yet become a problem, unless you're riding a bicycle alongside.

Instead of conventional city noises, Hanoi's modest background of sound comes from chirping cicadas, cyclo bells, and the whoosh of bicycle pedals. I never heard or saw an airplane, although one day I was startled to hear a helicopter overhead and felt a moment of panic. Like everyone around me, I stopped and looked up in trepidation, wondering what was happening.

Wide avenues lined with majestic palms and flowering flamboyant poinciana and jacaranda trees grace the city's old European quarter. Pastel-hued French colonial buildings with elegant wrought iron and mansard roofs recall the luxury of colonial life. In stark contrast, the rest of the city thrives in narrow streets with temples and small traditional Vietnamese houses, many with tiny interior courtyards. Trees spread their branches over the middle of the streets in a leafy canopy, screening out sun and showers. These areas bustle with life, overflowing from houses and shops onto the sidewalks and streets, as in other Oriental cities.

But Hanoi's charm is threatened. Work has begun on high-rise hotels in the center of town, where now only a few buildings exceed five stories. During my Hanoi stay only one building boasted an elevator, and that wasn't operating. Sadly, it is said to be cheaper to destroy the rundown French villas than to renovate them, so they are being replaced with concrete structures. Some of the giant old trees are being uprooted, for reasons I was never able to determine. Hanoi in its search for a better life for its people is about to stumble into modern times, and those who love the city worry it will leap unplanned and headlong into the chaotic modernity that has ruined so many once-lovely Oriental cities.

The French, beginning in the late nineteenth century, attempted to bring "home" to an

31

alien land by building their villas and public buildings in a wide range of French styles. There are mock French manors, which might seem more appropriate in the Alpes-Maritimes but, somehow, do not jar the senses sitting next to baroque Parisian bourgeois mansions, or spacious homes in the style of Paris suburbs. One entire section of town resembles a museum of art deco architecture; the pastel stuccoed villas display round windows, curved facades, and
Ill. 27-29 a starkness of line and decoration not found in other buildings.

There are even elaborate chateaux of a sort found in the French countryside, such as the former French Ministry of Finance, now home to Vietnam's Foreign Ministry. The Hanoi Theater is a near copy of the Palais Garnier, the nineteenth-century baroque Paris Opera House. Inside, however, inadequate maintenance and abundant rodent life were reminders of
Ill. 31 difficult times.

A number of early French buildings occupied by embassies and international organizations, as well as some official Vietnamese buildings, are carefully preserved. Many more, however, crumble in advanced deterioration from neglect and the relentless assault of tropical conditions. The desperate search for more living space in Vietnam's cities has turned once-gracious villas into eyesores with makeshift additions jury-rigged onto walls or sprouted within garden enclosures. Despite all this, the patina of age lends the old buildings a certain
Ill. 30 attractiveness, and abundant trees and verdant shrubbery soften the cityscape.

Vietnam's melange of religions reflects in Hanoi's architecture, with neo-Gothic cathedrals, Protestant churches, and Oriental temples and pagodas devoted to Confucius, Buddha, and Taoism. On nearly every city block may be found a tiled-roof Buddhist pagoda or temple dedicated to one of Vietnam's many legendary heroes, some with elaborate entry gates and courtyards. Along others, narrow passageways lead to unobtrusive entrances to small, carefully
Ill. 32-33 tended pagodas.

I was surprised to find that, in spite of the nation's grinding poverty, city officials have chosen to nourish people's spirits by preserving and tending to oases of beauty throughout the city, in the form of well-tended parks. Several small lakes and scores of ponds lie amid beds of seasonal flowers and rolling lawns painstakingly manicured with small hand shears. (I never saw a lawn mower in the country.) Here grandparents baby-sit, barbers set up shop beneath trees, lovers seek refuge from overcrowded homes, friends gossip, and teenagers gather in the
Ill. 36 evenings to play guitars, sing, and flirt.

In the heart of the city on a tiny island in Hoan Kiem Lake rises the gem-like Tortoise Pagoda, often depicted as the emblem for Hanoi. Not far distant, just beyond the inviting arch of a red wooden bridge, a handsome temple honors the Father of Medicine La To, the Genius of Letters Van Xuong, and the thirteenth-century General Tran Hung Dao, who three times
Ill. 34 defeated invading Mongol armies.

As my exploring continued, I found that Hanoi is really a collection of villages. Many quartiers are accessible only by narrow footpaths that wind past walled block housing and lead into open spaces containing communal water supplies – wells, faucets, palm-fringed ponds. Seven- or eight-foot-high walls conceal small gardens or neighborhood pagodas. Because few
Ill. 35, city noises intrude, it is easy, when strolling these small back streets, to feel you have suddenly
37-40 been transported to a remote country village.

Little material evidence remains of China's thousand-year occupation of Vietnam, from 111 B.C. to 927 A.D., except the architectural heritage of small, individual houses with curved roofs resembling those in China today, and the temple and pagoda complexes influenced by traditional Chinese style. Chinese characters still decorate Buddhist temples, greeting cards, the large red paper cut-outs pasted to walls on festive occasions, and buses transporting people to weddings or funerals. But most of Hanoi's decorative art, indoors and out, is
Ill. 41 uniquely Vietnamese.

Until the late 1970s a large Chinese population thrived in both the North and South – primarily in the cities. Recent improvement in relations between China and Vietnam, always difficult but totally estranged since the Chinese invaded in 1979, is increasingly evident in the street markets. In 1989 the border was unofficially re-opened to commercial traffic, and the Vietnamese prize imported Chinese consumer items, including apples (Vietnam grows none), porcelain, paint, clocks, velvet wall hangings, clothing, and the popular Chinese beer. Because the Chinese destroyed all roads leading to the border in 1979, these imports are carried by porters to trucks waiting several miles inside Vietnam. Work to repair the roads and railroad has begun.

Ill. 42

Colonial architecture is not the only reminder of the eighty-some years of French rule. French bread – not quite as crispy on the outside as in Paris, but very tasty – in the form of short baguettes, is stacked in pyramids and sold on street corners. Coffee shops paint "ca fe" on their walls (the Vietnamese language is monosyllabic), and many other French words have been absorbed into the language. Old men wear blue berets, as do many women and young men in the cold winter months. Children set out for school with the same sort of book bags strapped to their backs as have generations of French schoolchildren. A visiting Frenchwoman noted for me that Vietnamese women knit in the unique French manner, probably a legacy from earlier generations taught by nuns. French concrete bunkers lie scattered around the country, at intersections of roads or rivers, reminders of the first Indochina war.

Ill. 43

Most older people in the cities speak French, such as one retired civil servant who sits all day, six days a week, by a battered bathroom scale next to a sign hand-printed in French that says, "Stay healthy, weigh yourself." His face broke into a wide smile whenever I headed in his direction for my semi-weekly weigh-in, which I did only for the obvious pleasure it gave him. Although there were nearly a dozen people offering a similar service in downtown Hanoi, only once did I see anyone getting weighed. The Vietnamese are not worried about being overweight – simply getting enough to eat is a primary concern in a country where malnutrition is prevalent. Once, some of my Vietnamese friends whom I hadn't seen for awhile greeted me by saying that I'd gained weight. When I expressed dismay, they explained that among Vietnamese, "You seem to have put on weight" is a common complimentary greeting.

Because the United States did not occupy or invade the North, the only physical evidence of the American war in Hanoi is the result of the air bombardment. During the 1972 twelve-day Christmas bombing alone, one hundred thousand tons of bombs – equivalent to five Hiroshima-type bombs – were dropped on Hanoi and nearby Haiphong harbor. During my first flight into Hanoi, I had been perplexed to see the landscape still pock-marked by bomb craters, as if the B-52s had unleashed their bombs only yesterday. I learned that even though nearly twenty years have gone by since the last bomb fell, many of the craters have not been refilled because hand tools are inadequate to work the impacted earth of the crater faces. Most craters are filled with rainwater which does not drain away; some have been adapted for raising fish, but most breed only malarial mosquitos.

First-time visitors to Hanoi are amazed to find that the city looks so good. Hospitals, schools, and populated areas flattened by American bombs have been rebuilt, and residential areas do not show effects of the bombing because most private homes have been reconstructed in traditional one-story style.

American helicopters shot down during the war are lined up outside the Air Museum, located on a large avenue called "B-52 Street," short for its formal name, "Victory over the B-52s." In some parts of the city, fragments of the downed Stratofortresses have been left where they fell as memorials, or because of the difficulty of taking them away. Recovered parachutes still serve as awnings for sidewalk cafes or temple courtyards.

Ill. 44

American cultural influence is more pervasive, though not nearly so pandemic as in other parts of the world. The U.S. dollar is the only foreign currency accepted in shops and tourist hotels, and foreign visitors are obliged to pay all hotel bills in dollars. Many visitors express surprise that English has become Vietnam's second language. And, as elsewhere, blue jeans are a status symbol among the young. Camouflage jackets of the type worn by Americans in the

Vietnam War, and T-shirts sporting giant replicas of $50-dollar bills are available all over town. A fad among young men is the baseball cap (but I never could find anyone who had ever heard of the game of baseball.) Some stylish young women also wear caps in bright or pastel colors, but with large peaks and fuller tops.

Ill. 45

American disco and rock music (no heavy metal, yet) are popular throughout Vietnam. Until a few years ago, music from the West was officially frowned upon, but its proliferation has been impossible to control. Soon after my arrival in 1988, I was startled one evening to hear live rock music in mid-downtown. Following my ears, I discovered one of the regular free outdoor rock concerts underway in the large square in front of the National Bank – beneath a large, roof-mounted portrait of Ho Chi Minh looking down in seeming approval.

Because no television programs or movies from the West are shown (with two exceptions that I know of) in Vietnam, knowledge of American popular music originates with foreign radio broadcasts – the BBC and Voice of America – and via cassettes brought into the country, usually through Bangkok. Consequently, few American entertainers are well known. But when I asked my English class of Foreign Ministry staffers to write an essay on someone they admire, I was delighted by a surprise. As expected, most papers discussed Ho Chi Minh or various Vietnamese poets, but one was a long, enthusiastic dissertation on Bruce Springsteen.

In 1988 an exception to the ban on American films was made when *Gone With the Wind* (in a print, I was told, obtained through the Russians) was shown on television. Two years later people were still ardently discussing it. Also in 1988 the film of Eric Segal's *Love Story* was televised. So popular was the movie that a Vietnamese translation of the book became a best-seller, and a Hanoi musical stage production played to sold-out audiences. A few American videos of films such as *Platoon* find their way into the country, generally through the black market, but it is illegal to import them without permission and the payment of duties.

Massive Soviet aid during and after the war has left its imprint on Hanoi architecture in the form of monumental gray concrete block buildings, all unexceptional eyesores. A few Soviet consumer goods, mainly small appliances, were available in the state stores and on the grey market. With the increase in more desirable Japanese imports, the disintegration of the Soviet Union, and other factors influencing Vietnamese economics, changing marketplace dynamics are inevitable.

The Vietnamese considered all Soviet products to be shoddy, and only bought them if nothing else was available. Caviar and canned goods made their way into the street markets, via the Soviet compound's equivalent of a U.S. military base or post exchange (PX), and were snapped up by the international community. The Russians occupied their own large compound, away from the international community. A Soviet diplomat told me there were then about 5,000 Soviet technicians, advisers and diplomats in Hanoi. Not well-liked, the Soviets were the object of jokes behind their backs; Vietnamese complained of their drinking too much (mostly cheap local vodka) and their arrogant treatment of the local people. Like those of the rest of the world, Vietnam's relations with the successor states of the Soviet Union pose unique challenges.

Suburbs and the Surrounding Countryside

The Red River (it really is red, or reddish brown) flanks Hanoi's east and northern limits but, unlike the rivers of Paris, Vienna, or Budapest, it is not an integral part of the city. The presence of high, protective dikes makes it possible to live in Hanoi and never even see the river, except when crossing a bridge to leave the city. Just beyond the dikes begins the countryside.

Suburban districts to the north and west sustain villages that specialize in particular occupations, such as flower-growing, papermaking, manufacturing incense sticks and firecrackers, and hand crafting wooden furniture. To the south and southwest lie Hanoi University and various institutes of higher learning and research. Here, too, is the city's small industrial area, with factories that make bicycles, rubber, batteries, soap, and tobacco products. East of the Red River lies a new business quarter adjacent to the obsolete air defense field, Gia Lam.

Ill. 46

The suburbs yield suddenly to a countryside remarkable for its scenic variety and heart-catching beauty. Everywhere water molds the landscape and frames it with lakes, ponds, rivers, and canals. Some sixty miles to the east, in the Gulf of Tonkin lies the amazing Bay of Ha Long. Here, in romantic vistas which have inspired generations of painters, more than 3,000 limestone islets jut out of the tranquil azure water.

Ill. 47-50

Rural villages are walled in the northern part of Vietnam (a practice less common in the South) and even the smallest hamlet boasts at least one pagoda or temple, maintained as carefully as the inhabitants can afford. Christian churches dot the countryside, particularly south of Hanoi, which was the center for French Catholicism during the colonial period. Unfortunately, many churches fell into ruin and disuse after more than half the North's Catholics moved to the South in 1954, when the country was temporarily divided by the international Geneva Accords. Several hours south of Hanoi sprawls the wondrous cathedral complex of Phat Diem with its mixture of Vietnamese, Gothic, and Islamic architecture, designed and built under the direction of a Vietnamese bishop at the end of the nineteenth century. The cathedral is well-maintained, and masses are regularly celebrated.

Ill. 51-57

A Flourishing City Life

Much of Hanoi life is lived on the sidewalks, partly because the acute housing shortage forces people to live in an average space of some two square yards per person. Living quarters are usually dark, with only one small window per room. Electricity is expensive and undependable, so it is frequently more pleasant to be outside. The absence of glass windows (only wooden shutters protect from the weather) encourages easy conversation between those inside and passers-by. But there's something else: I think Hanoians spend a lot of time outside because they are naturally gregarious.

Families cook on charcoal braziers in front of their doorways, and eat squatting or sitting on tiny stools at a small table. I never got over my feeling of kinship to Lemuel Gulliver, because almost everything in the country is fashioned on such a small scale: doorways are smaller than in the West, stools and bamboo chairs are only four to six inches off the ground, tables only a foot high and sometimes not much wider; spoons look like miniature replicas of the real thing; teacups are not much larger than thimbles.

In the non-French Colonial sections of town, the only water source is faucets set into sidewalks. Vegetables, rice, dishes, laundry, feet, hands, and heads are washed outside, even on the coldest days. I shivered sympathetically when I saw people washing themselves in near-freezing temperatures or working bare-legged up to their thighs in frigid water in the rice paddies all day. I wondered how they could possibly stand it. I felt even worse when they would smile and wave at me as bundled up from head to toe I passed by on my bicycle on my way to work at the Institute. These folks are tough.

Commerce is also conducted in the streets. Since late 1986, when the government dropped its ban on free enterprise, Hanoi has reverted to its origins as a commercial and trading center. New small, family shops spring up daily in living quarters facing the street. Tradespeople without premises spread their wares on sidewalks. The proliferation of people selling things in the streets recently caused an annoyed Hanoi official to publicly complain that "Hanoi is turning into a street circus." Most of the businesses are pitifully small: a few homemade cakes or other snacks, a half-dozen packs of cigarettes – each cigarette sold individually, refills for the disposable gas lighters thrown away in the West, basketsful of plastic sandals, ribbons and sewing materials. Every fifty to a hundred yards or so, a bicycle repair "shop," consisting of a man or boy squatting on the sidewalk with a much-repaired tire pump and small, handmade toolbox, awaits the next needy cyclist.

When they're not in school or studying (always a high family priority), children are expected to work: boys mend shoes, act as porters, or hunker on the sidewalk patiently straightening out bits of rusted metal or nails with an improvised hammer or stone, or assist sidewalk artisans – carpenters, welders, and the like. Little girls struggle under the weight of smaller children, or sell hot tea, food, or fruit while sitting on a patch of sidewalk they've marked off as theirs. Women embroider and sew shirts and blouses by hand or on their treadle-operated machines, weave mats and baskets; and it is they who set up impromptu Ill. 58,60 produce markets on the streets.

From the Middle Ages, Hanoi's guilds of craftsmen and merchants grouped their shops on particular streets, and the practice endures today. Some streets are named for occupations: Silk Street specializes in embroidered silk and cotton goods, a counterpart to Tin Street, Straw Mat Street, Paper Street, Sugar Street, Rice Street, and Traditional Medicine Street. Grilled Fish Street has the oldest restaurant in town and was mentioned in a Somerset Maugham story. There are blocks where people sell apples from China, and special streets cater to lottery ticket sellers. On the corners of one busy intersection, several dozen blind people sell prescription medical supplies, including IUDs, most of which have been sent from abroad by overseas relatives. Both sides of one short street abound with vendors selling only sunglasses, while on another are arrayed a startling variety of Chinese porcelains. To my disappointment, the only place to buy cheese was on a single street where five or six small stands huddled on the Ill. 82 sidewalk, selling butter and bland, ersatz cheddar imported from Russia.

There are also some gray market items (taxes have not been paid on them): bargain Russian caviar, Coca Cola, Western whiskey and French wine, imported tinned fish, and marmalades. Soon after a French ship carrying supplies to the French embassy in Hanoi had an "accident" Ill. 59 in a storm off the local coast, the gray market area was awash with bottles of French champagne. Such "accidents" are apparently not uncommon.

One of the wonders of Hanoi is the traffic, a constant topic of conversation for visitors and locals alike. Officials estimate that one-third of Hanoi's three million people own bicycles: during rush hours that estimate seems modest indeed. A recent report indicated that ninety-three percent of Hanoi's passenger traffic rides astride bicycles and motorcycles, most of which carry two people, sometimes three.

Each Vietnamese I met, from cyclo driver to ranking politician, seemed genuinely concerned when they learned that my principal transportation was a bicycle. Recovering from their initial surprise, most expressed admiration that I chose to risk life and limb "out there among the people." When I was introduced to Foreign Minister Nguyen Co Thach at a Ill. 62 reception and identified myself as the American teaching his Ministry employees, he smiled and said, "Ah, yes. I've heard of you. You are my English teacher on a bicycle."

Apprehension was justified. My shins routinely bore scars of diverse vintage, badges of minor traffic skirmishes, and more than once I found myself sprawled in the roadway. After one especially nasty fall, I reflected that I might be a bit old to be picking myself up off the streets of Hanoi.

Having read about the extraordinary discipline of Northern soldiers and civilians during the war, I stared in disbelief at my first sight of Hanoi traffic – a chaotic melee of machines and people unlike anything I'd ever seen before, even in Paris. The city's three or four traffic lights serve only as decorations. Abrupt and unsignalled left-hand turns are routinely made from far right lanes, vehicles grandly veering across the paths of dozens of cyclists. When railroad barriers in the center of town are lowered, cyclists blithely lift them up for traffic to ignore the approaching train. Even more astonishing to see in this totalitarian society was the way people treated the rare policeman. When an officer did attempt to reprimand a cyclist or driver, he was smiled at indulgently or simply ignored. I spoke of this to my classes and they, in turn, were open-mouthed when I explained that in America everyone stops at red lights or on instructions from a policeman. And they questioned me closely about the strange notion of punishment for dangerous driving.

For the veritable anarchy of Hanoi streets, the absence of traffic laws is partly to blame, as is the fierce individualism of the Vietnamese. Perhaps the people's vaunted wartime discipline dissipated with the signing of the peace treaty, or maybe it never ran to municipal street transport at all. Battling the traffic each day, I saw scores of accidents, some serious, several fatal. Consequently, whenever I met someone of influence, at diplomatic receptions usually, I asked why dangerous drivers were not punished. The looks I got were about what I might expect at a Washington cocktail party if I suggested repealing the Bill of Rights.

Hanoi's public transport system is so inadequate as to be irrelevant. Several rusty trolleys left over from the 1930s rumble through town on patched tracks, and a few leaning buses lurch through the streets. Rickety old trucks flounder about, always in the middle of the road where they jockey for space with motorcycles, motorbikes, and motorscooters. There are no licensed taxis, and private automobiles – imported, expensive, extremely rare – have only recently been permitted.

Traffic problems are compounded by swarms of various moving objects, in addition to bicycles and motor vehicles: oxen lumber with overladen carts, women balance heavy baskets on their heads or on the ends of bamboo shoulder-poles, humans strain as dray animals. Pedestrians appear to be trained from the cradle to avoid eye contact with anyone in or on a wheeled vehicle, and most survive miraculously. Drivers of motor vehicles use the wrong side of the street and look only straight ahead. People don't even expect them to slow down, much less stop at intersections. ("No one has brakes in this town.") Nightfall brings added difficulties. The countless bicycles, none of which carries a light of any kind, are so many darting shadows under the dim or non-existent street lights. Motor vehicles of every sort have only one working light or none at all; Westerners living in Hanoi to say they can identify foreign embassy automobiles from a long distance off at night: they're the cars with two lights.

Somehow amidst the chaos calm prevails. Bicyclists pedal slowly, and sometimes chat or flirt with neighboring cyclists. Young men and women ride two or three abreast with their arms around one another's shoulders. The constant cut-offs and near-misses generally bring only a withering look, but I mentally cursed offenders in no uncertain terms, and from time to time actually yelled, "Look out, you fool!" in English. The Vietnamese, not given to public expression of their feelings, found my outbursts curious. Bicycle parking lots are set up on sidewalks or streets, and cyclists are given a numbered square of paper whose number is written in chalk on the bicycle seat.

Ill. 61,63

Warm Hanoi nights are magical, and the town takes on the air of a rural village, the streets glowing softly in the yellow-gold of low-wattage incandescent bulbs. Although most people begin their days at dawn or earlier, many don't go inside at night until the last bit of amusement has been drained from the streets. Flickering amber kerosene lamps, more reliable and less costly than electric lights, dot the sidewalks and glow through pane-less windows. Many private shops and cafes outline their windows and doors, and sometimes even potted plants, with tiny white or multi-colored electric lights. Day and night alike echo with the pervading melody of chirping cicadas.

Each evening shortly after sunset Hanoi's army of women street cleaners descends on the day's refuse with wheelbarrows and long, handmade twig brooms. The sound of their bells reminds householders to bring out their trash and garbage, which will be carted to specific corners and picked up by trucks, after first being carefully picked over by a handful of old women who wait around every night. A United Nations Development Program (UNDP) official in Hanoi told me of a recent report by visiting experts which cited Hanoi as holding the dubious honor of having "the purest garbage in the world." Nothing that could possibly ever be of any use is thrown away. Coca Cola and beer cans are plucked from embassy trash bins, their tops cut off, and the cans sold in the streets as drinking vessels; glass jars too are desirable consumer items.

Bell sounds emanate from the cyclos in the evening, announcing their passage through traffic, and because their heavy loads and lack of brakes preclude sudden stops, everyone yields them the right-of-way. The night air carries music from cassette players in homes, restaurants, cafes, and shops. From time to time, traditional music is played on overhead speakers affixed to electricity poles throughout the city. Unlike the din on the streets in many Ill. 64 Mediterranean or Latin American cities, Hanoi's sounds are generally muted.

The loudspeakers serve several functions in a country of more than sixty-seven million where only about two million possess radios, a much smaller number own television sets, where newspapers and magazines are too expensive for most people to buy, and watches and alarm clocks are luxuries. At 5:00 or 5:30 a.m., the speakers awaken residents with exercise music, followed by announcements of local or national interest, and then by Vietnamese popular music.

Loudspeakers are not the only early-morning sounds. In the center of town, carillon bells play short tunes that reminded me of nursery rhymes, at 6 a.m., noon, and 6 p.m. In some quarters, bells in Buddhist temples sound at 5:30 a.m. and, just before the crack of dawn, roosters may be heard in every neighborhood. At 6:30, kettle drums call children to class; later, in from recess. The drum rolls are always the same, beginning with exaggeratedly slow thumps that increase in intensity and speed to end in a frenzy of banging. When they stop, chattering children quiet down and march into their classrooms. I never had use for the alarm clock I'd carried halfway round the world.

Although not so predictably timed, other sounds are integral to Vietnamese life. Firecrackers of every size are set off at the slightest excuse. The traditional reason, explained my Hanoi friends, is that the noise wards off evil spirits, "in order to leave room for happiness." No holiday, wedding, birthday, or other special family occasion is complete without them. They also punctuate passing an exam, receiving a good grade on an essay, attaining a promotion, or just feeling good.

The most popular firecracker form is a string with fifty to one hundred or more small crackers, primed for consecutive explosions. Small powder loads are interspersed with much larger ones, making big bangs even more startling: tat-tat-tat-tat-BOOM! Some create as much noise and vibration as artillery fire. My windows rattled and floors shook when children set off firecrackers behind the elementary school located across the canal more than a football field length's distance from my apartment. But during the months before celebration of the lunar new year, at Tet, the firecracker truly comes into its own. The larger firecrackers – six or more inches in length – appear for sale in the shops and streets. Some very special firecrackers are several feet long.

Hanoi shimmers with distinctive scents and smells. Intriguing the nose and helping to keep the mosquitoes at bay, the fragrance of sandalwood and jasmine incense burning at ancestral altars or on the streets mingles with the aromas of spicy fish cooking on charcoal braziers. Everywhere hangs the pungent tang of nuoc mam, the fermented fish sauce without which a true Vietnamese meal is impossible. Many foreigners at first find the odor unappealing, but Ill. 65 soon enough it becomes part of the scene.

Unfortunately, the sights, sounds, and smells of Hanoi will soon give way to the noise and pollution that will surely accompany the economic progress already begun, and so badly needed. With the government encouraging tourism and increased commerce and industrialization, the Old World aspect of Hanoi will certainly diminish or disappear altogether. Trucks, buses, and automobiles will render the cyclos obsolete, and their departure will signal the beginning of the end of Hanoi's charm.

History

"The universe was created,
And the royal city was built.
Here gather mandarins in gorgeous dress,
Court music resounds
Culture and honor blossom.
The sky is filled with spring air, the whole universe gleams,
Like a solid pillar amidst the affluent nation stands the capital."

Nguyen Gian Thanh, 1508

Ancient Vietnam

As early as the seventh century B.C., in what is now known as the Dong-son era, the first independent Vietnamese kings, the Hung, united the various bronze-using cultures of northern Vietnam. In 111 B.C., after many attempts the Chinese Han dynasty conquered the kingdom and annexed it, calling it "Annam," the "Pacified South."

Chinese occupation was marked by repeated uprisings, including a briefly successful revolt led by two women generals, the Trung sisters. The Vietnamese made life so miserable for their occupiers that Chinese officials considered a posting to Vietnam as dreadful as twentieth-century Russians regard being sent to Siberia. One early Chinese emperor complained: "The Vietnamese are indeed not a reliable people. An occupation does not last very long before they raise their arms against us and expel us from their country." Ill. 67

Vietnam regained its independence from the Chinese after more than a thousand years of occupation, in A.D. 927. Through sheer stubbornness they had managed to retain their language and customs, defying Chinese efforts to transform them into Chinamen. Ly Thang Kiet established the Vietnamese capital, then called Thang Long, at Hoa Lu, about sixty miles south of today's Hanoi. In 1010, King Ly Thai To moved to the present site, where he embarked on an ambitious building program to make his capital into a sumptuous city. Ill. 69

Before the end of the eleventh century, three concentric walled areas encircled the Forbidden City at their center, surrounded by the Royal City, which was ringed round in turn by the Commoner's City. The innermost Forbidden City lay behind a moat linked to the Red River by a series of canals. The Forbidden City was considered so sacred that access was denied to everyone not specifically invited by the king himself, including his immediate family. The Royal City was reserved for the king's family and courtiers, and the Commoner's City was occupied by mandarins (the traditionally highly-educated government bureaucrats), officers, soldiers, and the common people, in a configuration that endured until the French took control of Hanoi in 1862. Ill. 66,68

Hanoi became an impressive city. According to one eleventh-century Chinese historian, "the main palace was a vermilion lacquered, wooden four-story building with columns adorned with gold painted dragons, dancing fairies and engraved ibis." Sculptured gardens, pools and lotus ponds, "whose flowers scented the air in summer" abounded. By the twelfth century, eight more elaborately decorated palaces and three more pavilions inside the Royal City were added, including the Pavilion of Fairies whose "upper story was covered with gold tiles, the lower with silver." Curved roof tiles, some clad in gold, silver, and white enamel, were engraved with roses, dragons, and phoenixes.

During the Ming dynasty, in 1406 China again captured and destroyed Hanoi and systematically set out to deny the Vietnamese their culture. Throughout a twenty-year occupation, the Chinese carried off all Vietnamese books and works of art; what they didn't carry off, they destroyed. In 1428 the guerrilla leader Le Loi crushed the Chinese decisively, and became Vietnam's greatest emperor. Le Loi changed the capital's name to Kong Kinh, which Westerners later pronounced and spelled as Tonkin – the name used for northern Vietnam – and restored the city to its former splendor.

Social and political turbulence struck again near the end of the eighteenth century. In 1786 the capital's palaces and citadel were destroyed when the Tay Son peasant insurrection raged over Vietnam. In late 1788 the Chinese once again invaded and captured Hanoi, but in January 1789 they were defeated by the Tay Son rebel, General Quang Trung, at the battle of Dong Da in a southern suburb of Hanoi. The Chinese did not attempt another invasion until Ill. 70 nearly 200 years later.

At the beginning of the nineteenth century, southerner Nguyen Anh conquered Hanoi, then moved the capital to Hué, in the southern part of Central Vietnam. The Chinese refused to recognize the new capital, and sent their emissaries only as far as Hanoi, forcing the Nguyen king and court dignitaries to travel to Hanoi to meet them. In 1820, angered by this indignity and the failure to subdue Hanoi's resentment against him, the Nguyen emperor ordered Hanoi's destruction. Even the citadel walls were razed, supposedly because they were higher than those at Hué. In 1848 a succeeding emperor ordered the demolition of Hanoi's remaining palaces and the transfer to Hué of all Hanoi's objets d'art. Later, as consolation to the North, the Nguyens built another, smaller citadel, of which only the Flag Tower remains.

Colonial Vietnam

Replicating a common pattern of imperialism, European colonists in Hanoi were preceded by traders and missionaries. By 1680 the Portuguese, Dutch, English, and French had all established trading posts in Hanoi. Bickering among themselves and opposition by the Vietnamese soon made the European enterprises unprofitable. By 1700 the only Europeans remaining were Catholic missionaries, who were obliged by the Vietnamese to live in designated concession areas bordering the Red River.

France, however, was determined to develop a colony in Southeast Asia and by 1882 had forcibly taken control of all Vietnam. In 1902 Hanoi became the seat of government for Indochina, which was to include Vietnam, Cambodia, and Laos. For governance, the country was divided into three parts: Tonkin in the North and Annam in the Center were ruled as protectorates; Cochin China in the South became a colony, with Saigon as its capital.

In spite of successive destructions that had preceded them, when the French took over Hanoi it was a picturesque city. They quickly razed great parts of it, however, in order to create a "Paris of the East." To accommodate their "European" quarter and army barracks, they demolished ancient monuments, pulled down the citadel walls, leaving only the North gate, the only section remaining today. To construct the Catholic cathedral and the present post office, French builders destroyed the Bao An pagoda complex, considered the largest and most beautiful in Hanoi, and the Kinh Thien Throne Room. Nearby they erected the Municipal Theater and large, ornate official buildings, such as the Bank of Indochina, with its Ill. 74 vaulted and coffered ceiling – today the Bank of Vietnam – near Hoan Kiem Lake. A colonial

Following a tradition
honored more than four
hundred years, at Bat Trang
just outside Hanoi this master
potter fashions art works
eagerly sought by collectors.

21 Perhaps a liitle awed by the visiting stranger, this infant is, says the author, "the only fat-faced baby I saw in Vietnam."

22 Sitting resignedly hat in hand on a park bench at the edge of Hanoi's Hoan Kiem Lake, this man was one of the few beggars met by the author during her stay in the country.

23 With pressurized water systems either inadequate or non-existent, gardens and fields are usually watered from watering cans on shoulder poles.

24 When a cyclo isn't handy, heavy loads are carried, even for long distances, on shoulder poles.

22

23

25 Goods of every kind make
their way to market in
flat-bottom skiffs.

26 Buses are an important part of Vietnam's transport system, and a typical arrival, like this one at Hanoi's Paul Doumer bridge, displays a bewildering cross-section of city and country life.

27 Echoing its Parisian inspiration, an elaborately worked mansard roof looks over the French quarter of Hanoi.

28 The converted home of the French governor of Indochina today houses the nation's Museum of History.

27

26

29 Art deco design and architecture enjoyed great popularity with Indochina's colonial residents, and numerous examples of the style remain today in Hanoi's French quarter.

28

29

30 Bearing its age with dingy grace, a French colonial villa wears today's cultural ornaments–garlands of bikes and motorcycles.

31 A near copy of the Paris Opera, Hanoi's National Theatre dominates a central square.

32 Not confined to famed countryside settings, excellent examples of pagoda design and decoration may lie around any city corner, like this one in Hanoi.

33 Recalling the European traditions of its French colonizers, Hanoi's Catholic cathedral rises in neo-gothic grandeur above the city.

30

31

32

33

34 As much a city landmark to Hanoians as the Eiffel Tower is to Parisians or Nelson's Column to Londoners, the Tortoise Pagoda occupies an honored site on the shores of downtown Hoan Kiem Lake.

35 The charming Lien Phi pagoda in South Hanoi is only accessible by a long walk down meandering footpaths.

36 In the fading light of dusk, a young couple enjoys the tranquillity of Hanoi's Hoan Kiem Lake.

34

35

37 Water traffic on Vietnam's rivers and canals is facilitated by a system of lift gate locks, like one near Hanoi.

38 Small retail shops flourish beneath the ornate façade of living quarters in an old section of Hanoi.

39 Often, ponds serve as the village's communal water supply, providing an opportunity for friendly conversations as well. The brick homes are typical of construction in the North.

37

38

39

Late on a peaceful, hazy
afternoon, bicyclists along a
northern canal have the
pathway to themselves.

40

41 Beneath a paper Chinese symbol for double happiness, guests at a Hanoi wedding celebrated at home await the beginning of the wedding feast.

42 Tangy imported Chinese apples await buyers at a street stall; comforters and pillows are stacked at a nearby stand.

43 Among other Parisian traditions happily retained by the Vietnamese is the street-corner vendor of fragrant fresh baguettes.

44 Difficult and expensive to remove, some wreckage remains, mute reminders of the war that raged from 1964 to 1975. Here

41

42

43

components of a B-52 protrude from a Hanoi lily pond.

45 Of the many influences arriving with the Americans, fashion remains among the most compelling, none more so than blue denim jeans and jackets.

44

45

46 Looking much like beached blond sea urchins, freshly made incense sticks cure in the sun along a Hanoi sidewalk.

47 Limestone, sculpted by wind and water into bizarre and fanciful shapes over millennia provide constant surprise and awe throughout the Hoa Lu region.

47

48 Its dazzling water and fairyland islets have become a virtual symbol of Vietnam's enchanting beauty, but Ha Long Bay in the Tonkin Gulf is also a rich fishing ground, plied by countless fishing vessels from villages along its shore.

49 On the rivers west of Hanoi, conventional short oars are replaced by longer sweeps, worked from the standing position.

50 Ponds, plentiful in the North, serve not only practical purposes, but enrich life with their tranquil beauty, as at Chua Thay Pagoda, some twenty miles west of Hanoi.

48

49

51 In earlier times, frequent invasions compelled villages to defend themselves, and many built perimeter walls. Often, only the wall's specially decorated entrance arch remains today.

52 As headquarters of Vietnamese Catholic diocese during the French period, Phat Diem Cathedral appropriately combines elements of both French and Vietnamese architecture.

51

52

53 Few European cathedrals
enjoy so spacious a setting
as this neo-gothic church
among the rice paddies near
Hoa Lu.

54 Abandoned by his flesh and blood successors, this stone French officer guards a gateway at Phat Diem cathedral.

55 Near Phat Diem a number of villages boast more than one Catholic church; here two substantial edifices face one another across the river.

56 Covered bridges possess a universal charm, whether in American New England or twenty miles west of Hanoi near the Chua Thay pagoda.

57 In rural villages, variety pleases the eye at every turn. Brick, stucco, thatch, tile, and wrought iron combine good-naturedly in this combined home and barn.

60 A popular item on Paper
   Street, blossoms are crafted
   in every color and shape,
   some replicating nature,
   some fancifully original.

61 In downtown Hanoi, even bicycle parking requires a system. For a few pennies, the cyclist receives a small piece of paper with a number printed on it: the same number is chalked on the seat.

62 Nguyen Co Thach, long-time Foreign Minister, when meeting the author for the first time, called her "my English teacher on a bicycle."

63 Each day she passed by on her way to class, the author found bicycles at this corner parking lot arranged in graceful curves.

61

62

Seemingly no load is too
ungainly for cyclo transport,
not even fifteen-foot lengths
of bamboo for construction.

Bubbling seductively at a
sidewalk restaurant, vats of
pho, the Hanoi noodle soup
specialty, lure diners with
fragrant aroma.

French guidebook identified the kiosk in the small park (renamed Indira Gandhi Park) in front of the bank as the Saturday gathering place for "tout-Ha-Noi" where women appeared in the latest Paris fashions, to be seen listening to band concerts.

Resurgent Nationalism

"Every man on earth ought to accomplish some great enterprise so that he leaves the sweet scent of his name to later generations. How, then, could he willingly be the slave of foreigners?"
Le Loi, rebel who became emperor in A.D. 1482

"The Vietnamese will to independence was too strong . . . to have existed without some intuition, reaching through all social classes right down to the seemingly crustacean politics of the bamboo-walled villages, that there was a special Vietnamese collective identity of some sort. The Vietnamese nation is, to put it bluntly, one of the longest enduring acts of faith in human history."
Historian Alexander Woodside, 1985

The French forever altered Vietnam by replacing its subsistence economy with one geared to producing surpluses for an international market, with the single objective of benefitting French investors. Small farms were confiscated to create plantations that produced export quantities of rubber, sugar, and rice on large plantations. Forced off their lands by confiscation or inability to pay the heavy taxes, peasants became a large impoverished class and many had no choice but to leave their villages to work as corvee labor for French mines and plantations. A French Inspector of Mines wrote a secret report addressed to the Governor General: "The peasants will consent to go and work outside their villages only when they are dying of starvation. We must therefore arrive at the conclusion that in order to extricate ourselves from the difficulty of recruiting labor, we must see to it that the countryside is plunged into poverty."

Such was the French *"mission civilisatrice"* in Vietnam. Vietnamese died by the thousands from overwork, malaria, dysentery, and malnutrition. At one Michelin plantation 12,000 out of 45,000 Vietnamese died between 1917 and 1944; French authorities kidnapped 80,000 Vietnamese to build a railroad, 25,000 of whom died in the process.

The French ruled with the help of a small privileged class of Vietnamese, but they were never able to secure reliable cooperation from the rest of the population. Rebels and suspects were imprisoned, tortured, and killed. Any who managed to escape or evade prison were pursued throughout Asia and Europe with inquisitorial zeal.

One who left in the early 1900s was the son of a dedicated nationalist who, while hiding from the French, changed his name to Ho Chi Minh, "He Who Enlightens." Eventually Ho Chi Minh would become the unifying force and inspiration behind the independence movement; modern Vietnam cannot be understood without recognition of the impact he had on his country. His memory today is revered by virtually all Vietnamese, even the most virulent anti-Communists in the South.

Ho Chi Minh, the Liberator of Vietnam

Ho Chi Minh greatly admired India's Mohandas Gandhi and his policy of nonviolent pressure for social reform through passive resistance against the British. But the young Vietnamese leader recognized from the beginning of his career that his country's colonial masters would never tolerate such benign revolutionary practices. Ultimately, he led a violent explusion of Vietnam's French overlords.

Vigorously rejecting the trappings of power, Ho Chi Minh exercised authority only by consensus and had almost nothing in common with other twentieth-century heads of autocratic states – no medal- bedecked uniforms, no self-canonizing books, no grand palaces, no personal wealth, no gratuitous violence. His apparence belied his position. By the time he became president, Ho was frail, his health broken from years in prisons and a fugitive's life, his clothing worn and mended but neat and clean. On the day he declared Vietnam's independence, he appeared for the first time before his people in a shapeless felt hat, an old khaki jacket, and rubber sandals. Subsequently, he almost always wore what he'd worn throughout his revolutionary days: a high-collared jacket, a khaki cloth-covered pith helmet, and footwear fashioned from old tires – "Ho Chi Minh sandals."

He was unpretentious and soft-spoken, with a manner everyone who knew him found genuine. A former opponent, French General Saintenay, said: "His simplicity was total. He did not grab power for himself, but exercised it collectively. The man incontestably wanted to be the Gandhi of Indochina." When Ho Chi Minh became president, it was assumed he would occupy the magnificent French governor's palace, but he refused to do so, saying that it offended his idea of what the revolution was about. He chose instead to live behind the palace in servants' quarters until he had built a small, simple cottage of his own design on the edge of

Ill. 76 a quiet pond in the park near the palace.

Although he identified himself with Vietnam's peasants, Ho was a sensitive man of culture, fluent in five languages and a serious scholar of the Confucian classics. Like most Vietnamese, he loved poetry and frequently communicated with his colleagues and others in verse. In 1941 he wrote Viet Nam's history in verse; and his prison diary ranks among the finest collections of contemporary Vietnamese poetry. French Minister Edmond Michelet visited Vietnam in 1955 after his nation's humiliating defeat at Dien Bien Phu, and wrote about meeting Ho: "He met us without any condescension, 'aucune morgue.' He was extremely obliging; the reception was very proper, and I was very impressed . . . I found him to be very cultured; he quoted Anatole France, Hugo, Zola, and Rousseau. Il était très français." In his autobiography, General Vo Nguyen Giap wrote: "The dominating feature in President Ho's personality was his selflessness . . . He always tried to arouse people's consciences, even when, as in the case of some people, they had hardly any left."

Beneath the meek facade thrived fierce courage and a spirit of adventure. Ho Chi Minh was heavily influenced by his actively nationalist father who supposedly encouraged him to find out more about the ways of the West in order to learn how to deal with the French. In 1905 the young scholar entered the prestigious University of Quoc Hoc in Hué, then taught in a private school. In 1911 he completed a course in navigation but, as a Vietnamese, he was only able to find employment as a cook's assistant on a French ship. Ho travelled throughout Asia, Africa, Europe, and North America, not to return to his native land until thirty years later. Like his hero Gandhi, Ho became the foremost nationalist leader of his country while living in exile for the same number of years as the Indian. To stay alive, Ho worked at odd jobs: in London he worked in the kitchen of the Hotel Carlton. He also worked in New York City and in later years spoke of having attended meetings of Harlem's blacks.

In 1917 Ho journeyed to Paris where he quickly became involved with the Vietnamese expatriate community, composed mostly of men who had served in the French army during WWI and who had stayed on in France to agitate for independence for Vietnam. Surprised and excited at finding in France the political freedom he'd read about but which did not exist at home, Ho attended meetings of various French Socialist parties to try to find a group that advocated independence for colonial peoples. He later wrote that he argued at these meetings: "If you do not condemn colonialism, what kind of a revolution are you waging?" He discovered that Lenin's party was the only one that promised to help colonized countries around the world to fight for independence, so he joined the Marxist Communists.

Thus, in his spare time from hotel kitchen jobs, he became a political activist, writing political pamphlets demanding freedom for Indochina. As the recognized leader of the Paris community of Vietnamese, Ho borrowed a suit and went to the Versailles Peace Treaty Conference. An admirer of American President Woodrow Wilson's strong stance for freedom and political independence, Ho hoped to gain attention for the plight of the Indochinese. But he left unheard.

Ho's continuing propagandizing activities in Paris soon forced him underground and earned him an "in absentia" death sentence from the French; and the long arm of the French Sûreté drove him into a clandestine life of name-changing and hiding. He left France in 1924 when he was invited to the Soviet Union for education and training in propaganda. In an effort to put the French off his trail, Russian newspapers declared Ho dead, much to the distress of his friends in Vietnam.

In 1929 Ho went to Bangkok, then to Hong Kong, where he officially founded the Vietnamese Communist Party. In 1931, cooperating with the Sûreté, British authorities in Hong Kong arrested him. Before he could be turned over to the French, a British Socialist and his wife helped Ho to escape from the prison infirmary where he was being treated for tuberculosis. Then he went to Shanghai, where he worked with the underground Chinese Communists.

In 1941 when the Japanese occupied Vietnam, Ho slipped over the China border into the north of Vietnam to organize guerrilla resistance to the Japanese. When he crossed back into China to contact anti-Japanese forces there, he was captured and imprisoned in China by Chiang Kai Shek's anti-Communist authorities. For more than a year he was marched back and forth through thirteen districts, usually shackled and wearing a cangue (a board around the neck, so large that the prisoner cannot reach his mouth to feed himself). He was confined in thirty prefecture and district prisons, never with adequate food or clothing; he lost many of his teeth, his hair turned grey, and he was near death when released. Ho Chi Minh's extraordinary prison poems, written in classical Chinese, are relatively unpolitical; many speak of acceptance, optimism, tolerance, and love.

On Watching Fellow Prisoners Sleep

In sleep an honest look on all faces is worn;
Only when people wake does good or evil show
Good and evil are not qualities inborn;
More often than not from education they grow.

Good-bye to a Tooth

You were, my friend, hard and unyielding;
Not like the tongue, soft and sinuous
The bitter and the sweet we have shared till now,
But this day each of us must go his way.

Near the war's end, in 1945 the U.S. government asked Ho and his guerrillas to help locate American pilots who had been shot down by the Japanese, on their way to or from China. The United States furnished him with weapons and sent an Office of Strategic Services (OSS) team, called the Deer Mission, into Ho's jungle headquarters to train and work with Vo Nguyen Giap and his soldiers. At one point during this period, Ho was ill and thought to be dying; an American officer probably saved his life by giving him the then-new antibiotic, penicillin. The Americans who knew Ho during that period consistently speak of him with affection and respect. While living in Hanoi, I met a member of the Deer Mission, Allison Thomas, who was visiting Vietnam for the first time since 1945. He met with General Giap who gave him a warm reception and he reported, "We reminisced about old times in Ho Chi Minh's jungle training camp."

Ho Chi Minh had long been a great admirer of American democracy, aware of President Franklin Roosevelt's expressed opposition to the idea of France retrieving her Indochina colonies after the war. Therefore he anticipated that the United States would help keep the French from returning to Vietnam after the Japanese were defeated. Ho even incorporated the opening paragraphs of the American Declaration of Independence into the Vietnamese Constitution, which he read during the Independence Day ceremonies on September 2, 1945. One of the Deer Mission OSS officers, Colonel A. Patti, was invited to stand on the podium with Ho at the ceremony attended by scores of thousands of people. An American warplane buzzed the podium as if in salute, a gesture which seemed to many to encourage Vietnamese hopes for American support.

As president, Ho Chi Minh guided his country through the French and American wars but died in 1969 before he could witness final victory. Aware of his people's adoration, Ho was careful not to permit a personality cult to develop, and tried to ensure there would be none after his death. However, Party leaders embalmed his body and placed it in a new Lenin-style mausoleum. Not until 1989 was the Party forced to publish Ho's will in its entirety, revealing for the first time his wishes. It read:

"When I am gone, a grand funeral should be avoided in order not to waste the people's time and money. I request that my remains be cremated. Not only is it good for the living from the point of view of hygiene, it also saves farmland . . . Let my ashes be divided into three parts, to be put in three ceramic boxes: one for the North, one for the Centre, and one for the South. In each part of the country, let the box of ashes be buried on a hill. Let no stone stele or bronze statue be erected on the grave. Instead, there should be a simply-designed, spacious, solidly-built, and cool house, where visitors could rest . . . plant trees on and around the hills. Let visitors plant memorial trees. With the passage of time, the trees will form forests which will benefit the landscape and agriculture. Care for the trees should be entrusted to local old people."

The French and American Wars

In 1945 Ho Chi Minh and his Viet Minh followers moved swiftly to fill the power vacuum left in Vietnam by the defeat of the Japanese. Their initial success in staging uprisings and in seizing control of most of the country was short-lived, for the French were determined to retake Indochina by force. Weakened from World War II, France was unable to accomplish its colonial reoccupation alone, and turned to the United States. Washington policy makers, fearing a Communist victory in Southeast Asia, authorized funding up to eight percent of the costs of France's Indochina War.

The French Indochina War lasted nearly ten years. By the end of 1953 the French were searching for a way to entice the Communist guerrillas out of the forests to fight a classic, positioned battle of the sort the Western military mind could understand, and which Western air power and artillery could dominate. French commander General Henri Navarre chose to commit his best parachute and Foreign Legion units to the Dien Bien Phu valley near the Laos border, hoping to lure Ho's army into a battle far from its base areas and beyond its logistic capacity to sustain. But it was the French themselves who were trapped, effectively cut off from land access so that everything needed for the battle, then very survival, had to parachuted to the besieged garrison.

Ho's military commander, General Vo Nguyen Giap, surrounded the French forces and solved his supply problem in a logistical exercise of epic daring and determination. Tens of thousands of Vietnamese peasants transported thousands of tons of munitions and materiel over treacherous mountain paths by bicycle, each peasant bicyclist carrying up to 400 pounds of rice, munitions, and even dismantled howitzers to be reassembled on site. Giap was soon bombarding French installations from the vantage of the high hills ringing the plain.

The siege, followed throughout the world via news broadcasts, began on March 13, 1954. Because all supplies had to be airlifted to the encircled garrison, when the Viet Minh destroyed the airfield resupply was limited to airdrops, made particularly difficult by near-constant fog. It was soon evident the French could not hold out for long, and they asked the Americans for help. President Dwight Eisenhower, however, was unwilling to commit U.S. forces to Southeast Asia without the support of the British.

After eight weeks of bitter fighting, on May 7, 1954, the French capitulated and 10,000 French prisoners surrendered to the Vietnamese. Dien Bien Phu ended the French will to continue the fight for control of Indochina.

On the morning of May 8, an international conference convened in Geneva to settle the political problems of Indochina. The Geneva Conference lasted seventy-four days and produced a set of agreements known as the Geneva Accords, under which the Vietnamese nation was to be divided into North and South Vietnam for two years, until national elections could be held to determine a united, permanent government.

Fearing a Communist victory at the ballot box, the United States created and supported in South Vietnam a government whose army, even though fully equipped and trained by the American military, was unable to put down the rebellion that broke out against it. The South Vietnamese government, backed by the United States, refused to permit the promised elections that would have united the country in 1956. In his memoirs, President Eisenhower recorded that it was common knowledge at the time that if the elections had been held, Ho Chi Minh would have won by a landslide.

Eventually American troops were sent to South Vietnam and fought the rebels. Many Vietnamese, however, were not interested in having one set of white faces exchanged for another, so U.S. troops from the beginning of their presence met considerable resistance and hostility. From 1961 the United States supplied support troops to South Vietnam in their battle with the Communist insurgents; and following the Tonkin Gulf Resolution by the U.S. Congress in 1964, the war quickly escalated. American troops numbered some 550,000 by 1969. The devastating offensive mounted by the Communists against the South Vietnamese and U.S. forces during the Tet holidays in 1968 severely discredited the previously optimistic U.S. military reports, and American domestic opposition to the war so intensified that President Lyndon Johnson chose not to stand for reelection.

In a national political confrontation of profound gravity, the American public eventually became disenchanted with what came to be seen as an immoral or unwinnable war, and President Richard Nixon was forced to withdraw the nation's armed forces from Vietnam. American troops left Vietnam after the signing of a peace treaty in early 1973. The last American advisors, civilians, and embassy staff stayed on until 1975, when the North captured Saigon and reunited the country.

But Vietnam was not to enjoy peace. After the Americans left, the Vietnamese were threatened on two fronts. Conflict between Vietnamese and Cambodian Communists on their common border began almost immediately, as Pol Pot's Khmer Rouge tried to reclaim portions of South Vietnam that had been part of the Khmer Empire in the fifteenth century. Finally, at the end of 1978, to neutralize this threat Vietnam invaded Cambodia, drove the genocidal Khmer Rouge Communist regime from power, and installed Hun Sen – a Cambodian Communist sympathetic to Vietnam – to head the Cambodian government. China and the United States aided the forces of the Khmer Rouge and the anti-government factions of Prince Sihanouk and Son Sann, prevailing upon Thailand to permit them the use of sanctuaries and supply routes. In an effort to regain power, Pol Pot began a guerrilla war against combined Vietnamese and Vietnamese-supported Cambodian troops.

China, angered at Vietnam's close ties to the Soviet Union and the deposing of their protégé, Pol Pot, invaded Vietnam at the beginning of 1979, causing widespread destruction in several northern provinces before retreating in the face of the Vietnamese militia. China then pursued a campaign against Vietnam that was more than a series of border incidents and less than a limited small-scale war, which forced the Vietnamese to maintain combat-ready troops in the northern regions. Chinese agents sabotaged agricultural, transportation, and communication facilities, and daily harassment by Chinese artillery continued for another ten years. Relations improved after the Vietnamese pulled their troops out of Cambodia in September 1989, and the border was finally pacified and opened for limited trade. By late 1991 the various factions had negotiated a UN plan for peace, and following the return of Norodom Sihanouk from exile to head a coalition regime, Cambodia's political future remained problematical.

In the 1990s, for the first time in many years, Vietnam itself is enjoying a respite from foreign invaders. The Vietnamese hope it will last.

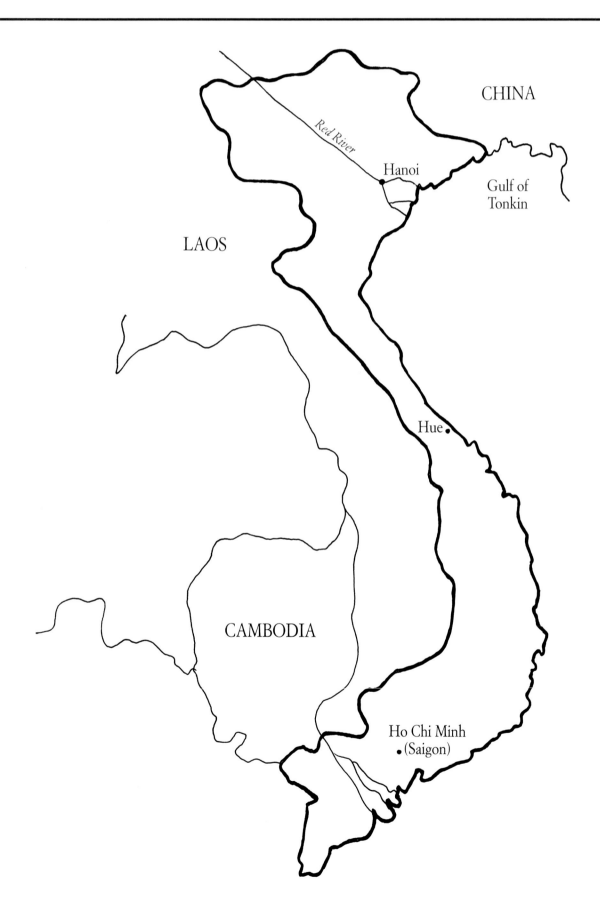

Today's Society

"The mountains and rivers of the Southern Kingdom are beautiful;
The place where the Dragon Spirit dwells is blessed."

Tseng Kun, ninth century. Keith Taylor, *The Birth of Vietnam*

Unlike many of today's developing countries, Vietnam gained a sense of cohesion early in its history, a cohesion derived in part from the profound effect of the land upon the country's political and cultural development.

Shaped by the Land

Vietnam forms the eastern portion of the Indochina Peninsula, adjacent to Laos and Cambodia. Shaped like a lazy-S, at its narrowest point Vietnam is less than 30 miles wide, and reaches a maximum width of about 360 miles; its coastline extends some 1,860 miles, most of it wide, sandy beaches.

Although Indochina is a compact geographic unit, vast cultural and historical differences separate the peninsula's three countries. The term "Indochina" embraces the region in which the early expanding cultures of India and China converged. Indian influence, spread by Indian Buddhist missionaries, ended at the mountains that mark Vietnam's western border. Art, architecture, music, and the easy-going life styles of Laos and Cambodia bear closer resemblances to the culture of the Indian subcontinent than to that of China. Neither Laos nor Cambodia ever possessed the fierce notion of national identity nor tradition of government and mandarin bureaucracy long cherished by the Vietnamese. As a result, neither Laotians nor Cambodians seriously resisted domination by the French.

Chinese culture, however, impregnated Vietnamese society. China's push south did not extend westward over the mountains, perhaps because the Chinese invaders encountered such strong resistance from the Vietnamese that they were not disposed to bite off any more. During Chinese rule, Vietnamese upper classes learned to read and write Chinese. Confucianism and the Chinese versions of Mahayana Buddhism and Taoism touched all social classes. Confucian obsession with a structured, ordered society run by mandarin scholars took hold in Vietnam and extended to strict hierarchy within the family. Throughout Vietnamese history, society revered scholars only below the king, and just above farmers, with soldiers at the bottom, beneath the merchant and worker classes. This societal tradition may have influenced the fact that during the war with the United States the North's leaders, scholars of literature and history, retained the loyalty of people in the North; whereas the South's leaders, principally military men or civilians strongly identified with the Roman Catholic Church were notably unsuccessful in generating or sustaining meaningful popular support.

Only about one-fourth of the country is readily arable, so the bulk of Vietnam's population of approximately sixty-seven million lives in agricultural villages scattered near the coast in the fertile deltas of the Mekong River in the South and the Red River in the north. These areas are rich in alluvial soil and enjoy abundant water resources that make them highly suitable for agriculture.

The mountainous areas outside the deltas support hardwood forests and diverse wild animal populations, including buffalo, elephant, and rhinoceros. The North enjoys large deposits of coal, iron ore, bauxite, phosphates, manganese, apatite, chromate, and tin. Offshore oil reserves extend the length of the coast.

Vietnam's climate remains humid throughout the year, and from July to November the North and Central areas are struck by typhoons that cause widespread damage to buildings, dikes, and crops. Northern summer weather is humid and hot, with temperatures of well over 100 degrees Fahrenheit; winter temperatures sometimes hover near freezing. The South's climate is extremely hot and humid during summer, but pleasantly warm in wintertime.

Not much more than a tenth of the country's population lives in urban areas, with about three million in Hanoi and nearly six million in Ho Chi Minh City – Saigon. Nearly two-thirds of the population is under twenty-one years of age, reflecting the effects of war on the older generation.

The People

The Vietnamese and The Minorities

Vietnam is one of the most homogeneous societies in Southeast Asia, with the ethnic Vietnamese majority, the "kinh," representing close to ninety percent of the population. The remaining populace includes more than sixty different ethnic groups, living primarily in the mountains. The national language, Vietnamese, is an Austro-Asiatic language spoken by some fifty million people in Vietnam, Cambodia, and Laos. It is monosyllabic with six tones, and exceedingly difficult to learn. The Vietnamese are believed to be of Malayo-Polynesian and Khmer (Cambodian) stock, descended from basically Mongoloid peoples who settled in the Yuan delta area more than 3,000 years ago. Around the fourth century B.C. these peoples began to push southward along the coast into the Mekong delta, forcing indigenous ethnic groups into the highlands, towards the Laotian and Cambodian borders. They eventually conquered the Cham empire that extended from east Thailand to the China Sea. Today Cham minorities live in central Vietnam, and in the South may be found minorities of Khmer Krom, of Cambodian origin.

The Chinese, who settled for the most part in large cities where they prospered in commerce and manufacturing, have been an important minority in Vietnam since the seventeenth century. In 1978, in the wake of the government decision to nationalize commerce and industry in the South, most of the nearly two million ethnic Chinese returned to China, although an estimated 700,000 of them remain – more than half in Cholon, Saigon's Chinatown.

The Montagnards

Vietnam's mountainous areas in the west are populated by diverse aboriginal groups, among them Nungs and Meos, named Montagnards by the French. These "minorities," as they are called by the Vietnamese, have jealously guarded their culture and customs, their stilt houses, colorful clothing and silver jewelry, and their own languages.

The mountains have been traditionally feared by the Vietnamese as "the land of bad waters and evil spirits." In turn, many highlanders fear and detest the lowlands and the Vietnamese, whom they consider intruders and exploiters of their land. Although the Montagnards make up only about twelve percent of the total population, they occupy nearly sixty percent of the country. As the Vietnamese moved southward, the Montagnards were frequently forcibly relocated. James Jones, author of *From Here to Eternity,* wrote: "Their position is almost exactly analogous to that of our American Indians a hundred years ago. They are hardly considered human."

Oppressed by the lowlanders, many Montagnard tribesmen greeted the arrival of white colonizers with relief, as potential allies against the Vietnamese. The French organized them into special groups to fight the Viet Minh rebels, and later the American Special Forces trained them to fight the Viet Cong. Many Green Berets became fond of the Montagnards, and admired them as reliable warriors. Ill. 77-79

I am unable to testify about the reception Montagnards might give Vietnamese who visit their villages, but on the several forays I made into Montagnard territory, we Westerners were met with the same generous hospitality we found throughout the rest of Vietnam. We were invited for tea and to inspect their communal stilt houses. They let us admire their beautiful silver jewelry and buttons on the women's jackets, and gave us demonstrations of their weaving skills.

Today the central government is making an effort to improve their living conditions by providing better educational facilities, improved health care, and agricultural assistance. Most Montagnards, however, continue to resist Vietnamese efforts to change their nomadic way of life, including their slash-and-burn agriculture. But many Montagnards have joined in government-sponsored efforts to preserve tribal traditions and handicrafts. Their lively music and dance offer a welcome contrast to the more subtle traditional Vietnamese dances and are very popular.

Unfortunately, ancient suspicions die slowly. A French friend of mine asked a Vietnamese woman why she occasionally locked her children in her house when she had to leave even for a few minutes. He replied, "Montagnards swoop down from their villages to steal Vietnamese children to help work their harsh lands, because their own health conditions are so poor that many of their own children die." A Western-educated Vietnamese parent told me, "When my children misbehave, I threaten to give them away to the Montagnards. It always works."

The Vietnamese

The Vietnamese are light-skinned, small, fine-boned, with coal-black straight hair (frequently kept dark by dyeing.) Seen on the streets, the vast majority dress in neat, trim, clean, freshly-pressed clothes. The fabric may be threadbare, but it is extremely rare to see someone looking dirty. A constant source of amazement to the foreign community in Hanoi is how the Vietnamese are able to stay cool-looking and unrumpled in their long-sleeved shirts during Hanoi's sweltering summer temperatures. Their apparent indifference to temperatures over 100 degrees Fahrenheit, with humidity near 100 percent, contributes to the aura of calm in the streets. No one looks uncomfortable in the heat, wipes perspiration from brows, or complains: it is simply accepted. Ill. 80

Compared to Saigon (now officially Ho Chi Minh City, but still commonly called by its prewar name), the people of Hanoi dress drably. But this is changing as more people – particularly the young – adopt pastel and bright-colored shirts or sweaters. Women wear close-fitting, tapered trousers and long-sleeved, fitted blouses, generally not tucked in; there are no dresses or shorts. (In Hanoi, I never saw a Vietnamese woman on the street in a dress, though it is not that unusual in Saigon.) A few young women wear jeans, and the majority wear the conical bamboo hats so practical as protection against sun and rain. The lovely *ao dai,* with its flowing trousers and overdress split to the waist, once the prerogative of the upper classes, is increasingly worn at formal and festive occasions in Hanoi – as it has long been in the South; but the garment is not yet worn on the streets in the North. Ill. 72

Since the official opening to the West in 1987, more and more young women have cut their hair, and a few have permanents. Although women in the South have long worn Western-style make-up, until 1990 Hanoi women did not wear make-up in public. Now it is not unusual to see it on young women. (It is, however, traditional for small children of both sexes to wear lipstick and rouge on holidays and special family occasions.) In Hanoi's many discotheques, though, stylish young women wear 1950s-style cocktail dresses or mini skirts; they arrive in their normal street wear and change into these "costumes" in the ladies' rooms.

Ill. 83

Footwear is usually plastic sandals, practical in rainy Hanoi. In the cold weather (and the winters are extremely cold and damp), socks are worn with the sandals. Cloth Adidas-type sports shoes are popular, but leather shoes remain a luxury.

Men and boys generally wear khaki, grey, or brown tightly-fitted trousers and shirts of a lighter color. The green jungle helmet is still the predominant headgear in the North, but baseball caps are becoming popular with all ages. Blue jeans, both trousers and jackets, are prized, and a Vietnamese yuppie would not be without them. Those aspiring to smartness sport sunglasses. Men and boys alike wear their straight, dark hair fairly long.

Peasants wear the traditional conical bamboo hats and loose-fitting trousers and tops; women's trousers are invariably black. Young rural women wrap a scarf over their faces to protect their skin from tanning; white skin is considered more attractive. In a recent poll published in a Hanoi newspaper, men of marriageable age said that one of the qualities sought in selecting a wife is pale skin.

Ill. 84

People in Traditional Hanoi

Lively historical contrast with today's fashions is found in the account of Ma Duan Lin, a thirteenth-century Vietnamese commentator who described Hanoi's citizenry: "The people wear their hair curled up into chignons; they go bare-foot, irrespective of their walks of life. So does the king, except on festive days when he wears gold necklaces, a yellow robe and crimson trousers. Women wear sarongs turned four times round the waist and black coats without belts. Men wear trousers under their tunics . . . they also wear iron or silver necklaces . . . in their hands they hold crane-feather fans to scare away snakes . . . on their heads they have conical hats made of bamboo sticks joined together by thread. The king uses carts drawn by men. Mandarins travel in palankeens make of linen, carried by two men."

Until very recent times, tradition called for stylish women to paint their teeth with black enamel – in a three-day process – in order to cover the unsightly brownish-red stains of betel-chewing. Many older women today still proudly display their gleaming black teeth.

Ill. 85

Differences between North and South Vietnam

An axiom holds that Vietnam is really "two countries." First-time visitors quickly note the singular physical differences between Hanoi and Saigon. Saigon abounds with Western-style hotels and a great many more cars, mopeds and motorcycles than its northern counterpart. Southerners are often better dressed, more stylish. Many women wear make-up and Western hairstyles; the men sport Western clothes. Saigon's trendy shops are more modern, better lit, and stocked with a far greater variety of consumer goods than is available in the North. Everything seems a bit brighter and more light-hearted than in Hanoi.

The North has historically been less affluent than the South, where the gentler climate permits three rice crops per year, and tropical fruits thrive year round. Saigon's port has always been more accessible to foreign trade than Hanoi, whose port at Haiphong is sixty miles distant. There is a residue of affluence in the South, a result of the American war when dollars flowed freely and the millions of dollars in remittances sent from overseas relatives.

Although Hanoi denies it vehemently, today the differences between people of the North and South seem little diminished with reunification. The people themselves acknowledge the personality differences between the North and the South, and don't seem to be as concerned about them as is the government.

Northerners are ethnically more homogeneous, whereas society in the South has been altered by the assimilation of large numbers of Chinese, the descendants of the Indian-influenced Champa empire, and the Cambodians. Vietnam's roots lie in the Red River delta in the north, and the Mekong delta is considered as their *terre neuve*. Consequently, the South is to many Vietnamese what California is to America's Eastern Establishment – new, brash, devoid of tradition and culture, not to be taken seriously.

Until the sixteenth century, when the Nguyen-Trinh conflict in Hanoi resulted in the flight south of the Nguyen court and its followers, the South held relatively few Vietnamese. The South represented a frontier for Vietnamese society and, as with the American frontier, those who moved there tended to be the discontented, the outcast, or the ambitious. Some were probably tired of the harsh Northern climate and others, because of demographic pressure, went to find new farmland and an easier life. An added attraction for some might have been that the frontier had few laws or rulers.

Anxious to learn more about personality and cultural differences between the North and the South, I asked my classes to make lists of the differing characteristics. At first many acted suspicious of my motives, and insisted that all Vietnamese were the same. I said that I thought in such an elongated country as Vietnam, with climatic differences, that must not be entirely the case, and cited the differences between various sections of the United States: Northeasterners, Southerners, Westerners. After I talked a bit about similar differences among the French and Italian northerners, they warmed to the topic and began to discuss the Vietnamese. Most of my students were from the North, but each class had at least one Southerner. I was gratified that they all agreed on the differences.

Southerners think of Northerners as unsophisticated – prudes and country bumpkins who have not had the advantages of contact with other cultures provided by the free-wheeling port of Saigon. This attitude extends to the government leadership; Southerners believe the North's Marxist ideology and lack of contact with the West have left them hopelessly out of touch with the rest of the world. Northerners berate Southerners for not being as patriotic as they are, and Southerners tend to agree with them. A saying has it that "Northerners fight against 'enemies' (French, Chinese, American) and Southerners 'co-operate' (for trade)." Political ideology has always been given more importance in the North, while the people in the South are more fascinated by mysticism, fortune-telling, faith healing, and magic. It is important to note, however, that although there are many Southerners who do not like the Hanoi government, they do recognize the North as the origin of Vietnam's civilization and admire the North for securing Vietnam's independence. Even Southerners refer to April 1975 as "the liberation."

Northerners perceive themselves to be more hard-working, frugal, durable, and intellectually superior to people in the South, whom they regard as spendthrift, frivolous, and overly materialistic. (Most Southerners cheerfully agree with this assessment.) Many Northerners would give almost anything to live in Saigon – which they consider a door to the affluent and socially liberated West. Others claim that, if given a choice, they would stay in the poorer North. One young Western-educated Hanoian told me he could not possibly live in Saigon because "it is too fast, too noisy." But Southerners love their raucous town and would not consider living in Hanoi, which they find "backward and boring."

Northerners are considered to be more tradition-oriented and resistant to change than those in the South. Most Northerners are proud of their interest in tradition and of their concern with the "correct" way to do things, but many admire the pragmatism of the South. One Hanoi official told me, "Southern attitudes are better."

Several people in my class contended that Southern children are better behaved than those in the North. They blamed Communist ideology which stresses loyalty to the Party and encourages children to criticize their tradition-minded parents, a betrayal of the Confucian doctrine of family authority.

Then there is Central Vietnam, generally considered to be part of the South. When I asked people about Central Vietnam's place in the categorizing of people's characteristics, I was told that neither Northerners nor Southerners trust people from the Center. Further investigation revealed that some resent the idea that people from Central Vietnam rather arrogantly hold themselves out as superior because they consider the city of Hué to be the intellectual and cultural capital of the country, and thus the most civilized region. Indeed, Hué is center for the study of traditional music and dance and the nation's classics of literature.

Although the Vietnamese acknowledge their regional differences, reunification has been difficult for other reasons. Southerners resent that the Hanoi government fired most Southerners in top management in order to give their jobs to Northerners whose qualifications were based mainly on party loyalty. Many Southerners became disillusioned when the North imposed Marxist rule on the Southern economy, even though Southern Viet Cong leaders had been promised by the North that they would participate in the new government and economic management. Southerners are angry that Hanoi has refused to abandon its rigid policies against Southerners who cooperated with the Americans, needlessly prolonging hostility between the two. On the other hand, the North resents the fact that people of the South passively resisted – and continue to resist – cooperation with Hanoi since reunification. Some officials continue to find it hard to forgive that so many Southerners made little attempt to hide their contempt for their unsophisticated Northern occupiers.

Nonetheless, Vietnamese are Vietnamese. The fact that over four-fifths of the population are farmers is a unifying force, as is the fact that, since 1954, so many families have relatives living in both areas of the country. New ties are also developing between urban areas, as the North becomes increasingly open to Western influence and acknowledges the need for Southern know-how in building a free enterprise economy. One Hanoi official told me, "You might say that the South really won the war, because now we are trying to emulate our Southern brothers."

Sectional character differences, however, are of little consequence in assessing Vietnamese society. Far more important are their common values: Buddhism, a sense of shared history, and the strength of family ties. In Vietnam, family loyalty is fierce.

The Family

When foreigners are introduced to Vietnamese, it is only a matter of minutes before the Vietnamese pose questions a Westerner considers personal. They want to know his family status, age, and details about the health and welfare of his family. Business meetings usually do not begin until inquiries are made about everyone's family. I was at first put off when waitresses sat down at the table to take my order (a common gesture of equality, I suppose), but before doing so, asked my age, whether I was married and had a family and, last, my nationality. (I now feel differently when American waiters introduce themselves.) I learned to carry snapshots of my grown children in my purse. Whenever I found myself in an awkward situation due to lack of a common language, I would take out my photographs. Everyone would break into smiles and common ground was established.

Throughout my stay in the country, every Vietnamese I met expressed amazement that I had made the supreme sacrifice of leaving my family to work as a volunteer in Vietnam. (In contrast, each Westerner I met expressed amazement that I would take an un-salaried leave of absence to work in Hanoi without compensation.) In fact, they made such an issue of my leaving my family for such a long period of time that I began to feel guilty – as if I didn't love my family well enough to stay near them. I seldom admitted that I live alone in Paris and that my three sons live half a globe away from me; I had swiftly learned that to anyone not familiar with American society, such arrangements would be neither comprehensible nor morally acceptable.

Age is important, for it determines an individual's "place" in society, and the way people address one another expresses such hierarchy. People cannot simply say "hello"; everyone must be greeted according to age and rank. A proverb says, "If you meet an old man, call him grandfather. If he is less old, call him uncle, and if he is your age, older brother." Young men and women are addressed with particular prefixes, and children yet another. (The egalitarian address of "comrade" is used infrequently in the North, and in the South I heard it used in humor or sarcasm.)

Confucian respect for age extends beyond old age to those who are dead. Veneration of ancestors is practiced by the vast majority of Vietnamese, who believe that after death the spirits of the departed continue to influence the living by acting as guardian angels of the home. The ancestral altar occupies a place of honor in most homes, carefully tended and decorated with incense sticks, flowers, fruit; frequently photographs or paintings of departed parents or grandparents grace the altars. Many Vietnamese believe that people who have no children to tend ancestral altars are condemned to be wandering souls, haunting the earth indefinitely. To discourage these bad spirits from entering their homes, people often place bamboo screens at the entrance; or mirrors are sometimes set on the roofs for the same purpose.

Family life in Vietnamese society has been profoundly shaped by Confucian traditions of the duties and obligations of each member of the family, with tradition dictating that the welfare and continuity of the family are more important than the interests of an individual. The extended family is a tight unit: grandparents, father and mother, children, and grandchildren, all usually living under the same roof. Sometimes parents have more than one married son living with them, but if they can afford it, today the second son will live apart. The eldest male rules, with women playing subordinate roles.

Family ties are strengthened by traditional rituals that center around the home: marriages, funerals, Tet, and anniversaries of ancestors' deaths. Although the government discourages extravagant wedding feasts and funeral celebrations as wasteful, most families continue to spend as much as they can afford on these festivities. The dowry has been officially abolished, but parents of the bride and groom still exchange lavish presents. Marriages and funerals are costly, with sumptuous amounts of food served throughout the day, musicians hired, and buses rented to carry family and friends between residences of the bride and groom, or to the burial grounds for funeral services.

Ill. 86-88

Second in importance to the family is the almost mystical bonding Vietnamese feel with their land. This bond is exemplified in the tradition of burying the dead in family fields, where they rest for three years before the bare bones are transferred to a Buddhist cemetery. The deceased therefore become a part of the eternal fertility of the fields. At the internment of a family patriarch that I happened upon, a peasant told me, "Our grandfather will be there with us when we are plowing the fields; he'll continue to be part of our family." Funeral rites include the wearing of white muslin hoods and tunics over regular clothing, and white bands of cloth wrapped round the head. White is the color of mourning.

Women

Some say that one way to judge a society is to observe how it treats women and animals. It is certainly not in the Vietnamese character to mistreat animals. Despite the Confucian emphasis on the obedience of women, historically Vietnamese women have been regarded as resilient, strong-willed, and notably more emancipated than their Asian sisters. Evidence suggests that Vietnamese society was once matriarchal; in certain minority regions today it is the custom for the woman to propose marriage to the man and, after the wedding, the husband moves to the bride's home and assumes her family's surname.

Women have figured importantly in Vietnam's history from earliest times, and some of the most revered legendary figures are women warriors, such as the elephant-riding Trung Sisters, to whom important temples are dedicated throughout the entire country. In the first century A.D., some twenty women were important military leaders, and during the last war women held forty percent of regimental command positions; a woman general, Nguyen Thi Dinh, was deputy-commander of Northern Army forces fighting in the South.

Vietnamese women today are better off than most women in other developing countries, although, like women everywhere, their position is not yet what it should be. The Vietnamese Constitution at least specifies equality with men as a goal, (which is more than many industrialized countries offer to their women.) Women have long had the right to keep their own names after marriage, and most of them do so. They can easily sue for divorce on grounds of incompatibility, and when dividing property according to the amount of work each partner contributed to the family earnings, housework is considered the equivalent of outside productive labor. Husbands are not permitted to initiate divorce proceedings if the wife is pregnant, but the wife may do so. Vietnamese women live without fear of being raped or coerced into prostitution (a problem in many Third World countries), and are free to plan their families through free birth-control devices and abortions. They are probably the only women in the world with guaranteed six months' paid maternity leave.

The dark side of women's lives is that they are vastly overworked. In addition to their roles as mothers and housekeepers, women provide approximately two-thirds of Vietnam's agricultural labor and a large part of the nation's heavy industrial manual work. The nastiest jobs of rice cultivation fall to women, and they make up over thirty percent of the manual workers in construction, engineering, transport, and communications. A common sight is a heavily laden cart, designed to be drawn by an animal, being pulled by a barefoot woman, sometimes very old. It is the women who carry loads of up to 180 pounds on shoulder poles, while cyclo transport of goods is the prerogative of men.

Ill. 71

In addition to long hours of labor outside the home, women are responsible for the housework, which is strenuous and time-consuming. With few exceptions, water must be carried from a well or communal spigot, sometimes up four flights of stairs, then heated. Drinking water must be boiled; wood, coal, or paraffin must be brought in each day because crowded housing provides no storage space. Clothes are washed by hand. Because there is no refrigeration, food must be purchased fresh every day. Most clothing is made by hand, and household gardens supply much of the family's food, even in urban areas. Children who are ill may require prolonged care because of the scarcity of antibiotics and other medicines. All this is women's work, although children and grandparents help. Husbands do, however, help with children, and it is not an uncommon sight to see men caring affectionately for children in the streets.

Ill. 93

Women enjoy educational equality (thirty percent of university graduates are women) and fair access to the professions, although there is undisputed discrimination in promotions to positions of power. Former general Nguyen Thi Dinh, president of the Women's Union, criticizes government leadership for not including more women in top government posts, as does Nguyen Thi Binh, who headed the Viet Cong delegation at the Paris Peace Talks. Women represent fifty-two percent of the population, but make up only seventeen percent of the National Assembly – considerably less than the thirty-two percent they had in 1975 immediately after the war (but still fare better than American women who, in 1989, composed only five percent of Congress.) A few women serve on the powerful Central Committee or in other high positions, such as Ngo Ba Thanh, who holds a law degree from Columbia University and chairs the National Assembly committee responsible for government economic policy. There are no women in the Politburo.

A Dutch aid official (a man) told me, "There is pernicious discrimination against women for overseas training programs. If left to their own devices, the government would not send any women for overseas or in-country training. We've learned to threaten to withhold fellowships if they don't include at least one woman." Another Western aid worker noted, "At a recent international conference on agriculture only a tiny percentage of representatives were women, even though they make up sixty-five to seventy percent of the agricultural work force. It's the men who get the perks in this country."

On the non-professional level, only men get the prestigious jobs, such as chauffeurs and truck drivers. Mme. Dinh believes Vietnamese women should be more militant: "Women do not push for their proper share of power because they are so exhausted from their daily work that they don't have the energy to lobby on their own behalf."

Today, in peacetime, the proportion of households headed by women remains extremely high. Because of high unemployment, many men leave their families to find work elsewhere, either in another part of the country or in one of the Eastern bloc countries as contract laborers. The government no longer attempts to dictate where or at what people must work, but even among professionals, husbands and wives are frequently forced to live apart for years at a time, in order to accumulate more expertise in their fields or simply to find a job for which they are qualified. Foreign Ministry employees at overseas embassies are not permitted to take their families, because the government cannot afford to provide housing; spouses may visit each other in foreign countries, but must go at their own expense.

The separation of husbands and wives has long been an accepted way of life. During the thirty years of war and the ten-year occupation of Cambodia, family life was seriously disrupted, leaving women to raise their families alone while working to support the family. Women occupied positions of responsibility in local or district government or enterprises; after the war some were reluctant to go back to their previous station of servility. Many became active in politics.

The Women's Union, a government-sponsored organization eleven million strong, has most of its members in the North, where it originated in 1930. Before 1975 there was no official emphasis on equality for women in the South as there had been in the North since 1954, and feminist attitudes have been slow to win acceptance in that part of the country. On such issues as family planning and health care, the Union promotes family reform by trying to raise men's consciousness about the sharing of household responsibilities, but so far with limited success. But, through its highly organized grass roots organization, the union has succeeded in focusing the government's attention on women's problems. Recently the government formally initiated an unusual policy to consult the Women's Union on all policy issues, whether or not specifically related to women.

Courtship and Marriage

Women, especially in the cities, have become more emancipated regarding the selection of a husband, a privilege traditionally reserved for the family. Courtship is low-key, and begins at a much later age than in the West. The teen-age years are still considered to be part of childhood, with the result that many young people do not date until they are in their twenties. Recent statistics show that early marriages occur chiefly in the countryside and among manual workers in the cities. Professionals and office workers tend to marry later, women between twenty-three and twenty-five, and men at twenty-six to thirty.

Arranged marriages are still the rule for many young people, especially in rural areas where marriages of convenience or expedience are the norm. A recent poll of young people on the question of "Requirements for Your Future Husband or Wife" revealed that, "Nowadays, the young have a more practical view of marriage, but they are also striving for greater values. The three things most valued are idealism, a decent profession, and good morals."

Once the selection of a partner is made, almost every family honors some traditional formalities. First the parents of the boy visit the girl's parents, taking a traditional round, red-lacquered box filled with betel nut and accessories for chewing. This makes the engagement official. Several weeks or months later the boy's family takes presents to the prospective bride's family, a legacy of the dowry custom. Astrologists are consulted before the wedding date is set, and frequently spiritual advisers are asked to give their opinions on the proposed match.

There is no "official" civil or religious ceremony per se, with the exception of the Roman Catholics and a few Buddhists. The family celebration gives the marriage its validity; the marriage certificate is obtained from the local People's Committee, either before or after the day of the wedding.

I was honored to be invited twice into a Vietnamese home for weddings of the children of a cyclo driver with whom I became friendly by helping him with his nearly non-existent English. Celebrations began at the bride's home early in the morning. In the cities, where most homes are too small to accommodate extended family and friends, if they can afford it the family rents a canopy – frequently red, the traditional Confucian color for happiness – which is set up on the sidewalk next to the family's home. At the weddings I attended, narrow tables and still narrower benches were crowded into the living room; music came from a cassette recorder, and paper decorations were tacked to the walls. A borrowed television set sat on a corner table, "for the children and old people." The wedding party and guests ate several sit-down snacks, later followed by a large formal meal.

I was embarrassed to note that although everyone else was drinking beer poured from a large plastic container, at my place stood two bottles of expensive imported European beer. My distress was amplified because I detest the taste of beer and never drink it. Needless to say, I sipped daintily at my glass (the others had cut-down coke or beer cans for drinking vessels) and hoped that everyone would think me very polite when I declined the second. Toward evening, everyone was shuffled outside to a waiting bus, whose windshield was decorated with a large red paper Chinese character for "double happiness". Men, women and children of all ages happily filled up the bus, while some of the young people followed on motorbikes. We were headed for the groom's home, where the eating and speech-making started all over again. Throughout the day, men and children set off fireworks, without which I'm sure the wedding could not have been considered valid.

Religion

I was surprised to find pagodas and temples very much in use, not reserved for tourist visits as were all those I visited in China. Browsing through them, I was impressed with the meticulous and lavish care they clearly received. Statues were painted and polished, altars stacked with food and other offerings, and floors so immaculate there was no worry about bare feet getting dirty.

Most of the pagodas and temples were staffed by nuns in brown robes (saffron is worn in the South) who were, without exception, pleased to have me visit. They, and anyone else in the pagoda at the time, always took me on tours of the pagodas, lighting incense sticks for me at the various altars, and pointing out interesting objects for me to photograph. I received the Ill. 89-90 same warm welcome on busy Sundays and festival days.

Religion in Vietnam is very much a family affair, centering around respect for ancestors. A Vietnamese historian, quoted by Jean Lacouture, wrote: "We have our own religion – that of Ancestors . . . we have remained Vietnamese and retained our loyalty to the memory of our ancestor King Hung Vuong [prior to Chinese occupation]. Our ancestors knew how to assimilate all three religions and to integrate them into a sort of unique vision of the world that Ill. 91 entered into the mores and customs of our people."

The Vietnamese have never believed in a single "true way" and, perhaps for that reason, the Communists never seriously tried to substitute Communist ideology for religion, as happened in other Communist countries. However, because both Catholics and Buddhists had been active in politics during the wars, the Communists sought to reduce the influence of religion by limiting the number of new priests and nuns and pressuring priests, monks, and nuns to lead a secular life "more useful to the people." Some who refused to collaborate were placed under house arrest or imprisoned, their pagodas converted to public use, and their holdings confiscated.

The vast majority of the population has continued to hold to their religious beliefs. In recent years the government has relented to the extent that it now helps restore religious buildings and even encourages religious ceremonies and festivals, in the interest of preserving Vietnam's cultural heritage, but tries to discourage what it calls "superstition." Notices at entrances to some pagodas command "there shall be no fortune-telling, no ritual dances (dong bong – spirit dance), no using incense sticks for telling fortunes . . ." All of which is blatantly ignored. I frequently saw old women telling fortunes in pagoda or temple courtyards, and during Tet 1990, spirit dances were performed in Hanoi pagodas, with no apparent objection from authorities. The burning of votive paper money or figures representative of humans, animals, or material objects, such as a car or motorcycle (supposedly to send them on to the ancestors), is illegal, but the figures can be purchased on Paper Street in Hanoi, if you ask for them.

Churches, temples, and pagodas are usually open every day, but are busiest on Sundays, the Vietnamese day of rest, when factories and offices close. (Private merchants and markets stay open seven days a week.) I read, and was told by Vietnamese, that there has been a resurgence of participation in religious ceremonies, even among educated young professionals. It is not unusual to see Vietnamese yuppies drive up to pagodas on shiny new Honda motorbikes, wearing sunglasses, bright colored jackets, skintight jeans, the women with permed hairdos and make-up.

Most Vietnamese identify themselves as Buddhists, but their beliefs and values also encompass Confucianism and Taoism. Buddhism, an offshoot of Hinduism, originated in India about 530 B.C. and expanded some seven hundred years later to Vietnam, where it found easy acceptance because its ceremonies conformed to indigenous folklore. Pagodas are dedicated to some aspect of Buddhism, while temples are dedicated to legendary heroes.

Buddhism teaches compassion for all living creatures, that man is born to suffer in successive lives, that unhappiness is caused by man's craving for earthly pleasures and material possessions, and that desire can be conquered by leading a religious life. The religion emphasizes physical and mental discipline, teaching that what one appears to be, one is. Therefore, a cultivated person loses face by revealing emotions, sometimes causing Westerners to refer to them as "inscrutable."

Taoism, which emphasizes the individual's relationship to nature and the universe, also had its origins in China. It urges followers to embrace *wu-wei*, non-action, letting things happen naturally and responding selflessly to them; "one should be like bamboo, bend with the wind." The concept of *yin* and *yang* recognizes a world of complementary forces – male and female, good and evil, difficult and easy, pain and pleasure, light and dark – which must be brought into harmony through acceptance.

Lao Tzu, a sage of the sixth century, is linked with the I Ching, which Taoists believe is a mystical guide to the Tao – or Way – the source of "truth" which can be found through examinations of the patterns of nature, mediums, geomancers (people who determine how new buildings should be oriented – important people today, even in such Westernized places as Hong Kong), sorcerers, astrologers, magicians, deities, and fortune telling. Fortune tellers remain popular in all parts of the country, and it is a common joke that theirs is the highest paid profession in Vietnam.

Ill. 95

91

When asked for one word to serve as a principle for the conduct of life, Confucius (551-479 B.C.) replied: "Perhaps . . . 'reciprocity': do not do to others what you would not want others to do to you." Rather than a religion, Confucianism is a set of precepts for harmonious living. "When the personal life is cultivated, the family will be regulated; when the family is regulated, the state will be in order; and when the state is in order, there will be peace throughout the world." Confucius did not think of himself as a prophet or religious leader, but as a teacher of morality, the correct behavior among individuals and between the state and individuals. He sought order and peace through reverence of traditions, and his concerns were with human society, rather than the supernatural.

Confucianism dictates that if a country's ruler fails his people he loses "the mandate of heaven," and citizens have a duty to change the mandate and install a successor. (The word for revolution in Vietnamese means "change the mandate.") Thus, cultural heritage validates the overthrow of any regime which does not act in the best interests of the people. Such a notion was probably at work in 1945 when Ho's new government was not formally announced until Emperor Bao Dai handed over the official seal of authority.

Vietnam's Roman Catholic churches are packed every Sunday, and many I visited had standing room only. An estimated six percent of the population are practicing Catholics. French, Spanish, and Portuguese missionaries established Christianity in Vietnam in the seventeenth century, and for a long time the new faith was tolerated as just another religious sect. However, in the nineteenth century, Catholics fell into disfavor for putting God above the new emperor, and for their suspected links with the foreigners who had become a threat to Vietnamese independence. After the French took over, the number of converts to Christianity increased, as people sought the favors bestowed on Catholics.

In 1954, having enjoyed favoritism under the French, many northern Catholics were concerned about possible repression under a Communist regime. An estimated 650,000 moved to South Vietnam, where they hoped to continue as a favored class under Catholic President Ngo Dinh Diem. Approximately 600,000 remained in the North where the Church was discouraged, but permitted to retain its link with the Vatican. The government did, however, strip the Church of its schools, hospitals, orphanages and, as with individuals, abolished the right to own property.

Protestant Christianity in Vietnam, almost exclusively evangelical, was developed primarily by American missionaries who worked with the Montagnards. Today there are an estimated 300,000 Vietnamese Protestants in Vietnam. Non-proselytizing Protestant organizations, such as the American Friends Service Committee and the Mennonites' Central Service Committee were active in Vietnam throughout the war and, after 1975, continued their projects from Thai or Laotian bases.

In the South, in the early part of the twentieth century there arose several indigenous religious movements that incorporate aspects of Buddhism, Confucianism, and sometimes Christianity. The largest are the Hao Hoa and the Cao Dai, which until the war controlled large areas like fiefdoms, each with its own army. Followers of these sects live mainly in the Mekong Delta area and number perhaps one million each. Like the ethnic minorities, these groups have resisted assimilation into regular Vietnamese society and remain as apart from it as is possible. The Cao Dai are perhaps the most exotic, with their wonderfully elaborate, candy-colored, baroque cathedrals and an eclectic pantheon of gods that includes Jesus, Buddha, Confucius, Sun Yat-sen (founder of the Chinese Republic), and Victor Hugo.

Religious and Secular Celebrations

The Vietnamese love any excuse to party, and all celebrations are accompanied by sumptuous banquets and exploding firecrackers, with everyone dressed in their best finery. (Alcoholic intake on these occasions is modest and usually limited to beer.) Numerous special days involve local pagodas: the anniversary of the founding of the pagoda, the birthday of the person who founded the pagoda, the birthday of the head monk or nun in charge of the pagoda, anniversaries of famous battles and victories, birthdays of national heroes, and the renovation of defunct pagodas.

In some cases the festivities are modest, with members of the community bringing fruit, food, flowers, and burning incense. Others are elaborate spectacles that attract hundreds or thousands of spectators, continue all day, and involve hired musicians and professional participants, as well as hosts of amateurs.

Even Christmas is celebrated in Hanoi. I was amazed in mid-December when colored lights began to appear all over town, strung over bushes and trees and outlining public buildings and temples. The Catholic neo-Gothic cathedral's windows, towers, and roof were decorated with strings of small white lights, and even the curved bridge leading to the island temple in Hoan Kiem Lake in the middle of town was illuminated. Downtown Hanoi was enchanting. On Christmas Eve so many people went to the main cathedral in the center of town that, in order to avoid injuries, authorities denied admission to those without advance reservations. Downtown Hanoi streets were filled with a crush of people, reminding me of Times Square on New Year's Eve. After visiting churches, young people went to the hotel ballrooms and dance halls, where advance reservations are also necessary. I've been told that Christmas in Saigon is even more festive.

Some observers believe the celebration of Christmas indicates more interest in Christianity than is publicly or officially admitted. I believe it is just a warm-up, or practice for Tet, an excuse for dressing up, setting off firecrackers, and having a good time.

Tet is far and away the most important holiday in Vietnam and it captures the country's imagination and attention for nearly two months every year. Tet celebrates the Lunar New Year, falling sometime between the 20th of January and the 20th of February, and is considered to be the harbinger of Spring. It is the West's equivalent of Christmas, New Year's, Easter, and Thanksgiving, all rolled into one. Preparations begin a good two months before the date, when women begin cooking special foods and sweets, especially sticky rice cakes made with young green rice. If possible, each family member will get at least one new item of clothing. Homes must be thoroughly cleaned inside and whitewashed or painted outside. Special woodblock prints from Dung Ho village are dug out of storage, or new ones purchased, to hang on the walls. Outstanding debts should be paid, and any hard feelings among friends or family patched up. Newspapers and magazines publish special issues, and temples and pagodas overflow.

Ill. 73,75

As Tet approaches, firecrackers are set off with increasing frequency, beginning at sunrise – or earlier – and streets become ever more crowded with people returning for the holidays. The pace accelerates, becomes frenetic. For the few days before Tet no five-minute period in the day passes without firecrackers booming. Several of my Western friends refused to walk in the streets during the last weeks of Tet because they felt the constant barrage of tossed firecrackers was simply too dangerous. I continued my peregrinations by bicycle. The streets were certainly extremely lively – and at times scary, as firecrackers landed in the streets from all directions. More than once I was startled off balance, causing me to question – yet again – my sanity in involving myself in such a wacky venture.

Ill. 94,96

A week to ten days before Tet, people visit Hanoi's suburban flower villages, or special cordoned off streets in Hanoi, to buy peach or apricot blossom branches, or miniature orange trees, the equivalent to Christmas trees. (Flower vendors keep their products fresh by filling their mouths with water and spraying the blossoms every few minutes.) According to Van, a doctor in my hospital class, "If there were no peach or apricot flowers or sticky rice cakes, there was no Tet in that family." Great care is taken in selecting the perfect branch since if the buds open on Tet day, the owner will have good luck in the new year. During one Tet I went with a UN official to a flower village to pick out our Tet branches, driving from field to field to find the perfect blossoms. As we should have suspected, we were not permitted to pay for the ones we finally selected.

Ill. 97

About six weeks before Tet, temporary kiosks appear all over town, their proprietors offering a dazzling profusion of special sweets, balloons, cakes, colorful woodblock prints, Tet presents, and souvenirs of Hanoi. Some booths offer simple games of chance or skills, such as wheels of fortune or tossing darts at balloons. It is the custom on Tet eve to walk around Hoan Kiem Lake just before midnight, and everyone is expected to set off as many firecrackers as it is possible to carry, or purchase.

During my first Tet in Hanoi, a group of European friends and I joined the throngs at the lake. Several hours before midnight the place looked and sounded like a battlefield, volleys and cannonades of firecrackers blasting away like a furious artillery barrage in a pall of acrid white smoke rolling in waves so thick that visibility dwindled to mere feet. Adding to the combat-zone illusion were all the trees and bushes stripped clean of their leaves, victims of the tradition that good luck comes to those who take "something green" into their homes at Tet.

On New Year's Day itself, a gentle silence settles over the city. Shops are closed, windows shuttered, the streets abandoned. Everyone is at home with the family. By late afternoon a few people venture out to visit close friends. In the cities, offices are officially closed for only three days, but no one seriously expects to do any business for ten days before or after Tet. Bureaucrats who must return after three days extend their holiday by napping at their desks, eating special foods, and drinking a bit of wine throughout the work day.

Two important secular holidays supplement the religious and traditional celebrations: Independence Day on 2 September, and Ho Chi Minh's birthday on 19 May. Both occasions are observed with parades, red flags and banners bearing revolutionary slogans printed in yellow – the colors of Vietnam's flag. The government sponsors free outdoor concerts of traditional and modern music and dance. Much speech-making and waving of arms occurs in the workplace, at spectacles, and on television.

Ill. 98-102

More fun is the children's Mid-Autumn festival. Its approach is heralded by the appearance of colorful hand-made cellophane toys for sale in shops and on the streets. Parents give children multicolored lanterns and masks for them to parade through their neighborhood or village. At the end of the evening the children go home to eat special cakes with their families, and to receive presents of home-made or purchased cellophane paper toys.

Cultural Life

"Fragrant are the soi and jasmine flowers,
Clever are the people in the capital city
Can you say that jasmine flowers are not fragrant,
That capital city people are not refined?"
Vietnam Studies, Volume 1

Staggering poverty has not dimmed a vibrant cultural life in the cities and villages. Even though the standard of living is far below Western standards, government leadership has made a priority of supporting and encouraging the performing arts, literature, and sports.

Free, or nearly free, classical and modern music and dance programs, both traditional and Western, are performed in theaters and the open air. Sports centers, marathons, and bicycle races, where winners are delighted to receive T-shirts as prizes, thrive. Classical and modern theater groups, puppet theaters, and circus troupes abound, and authorities now encourage the elaborate religious festivals and ceremonies at pagodas and temples. A lively arts scene flourishes, with numerous painting and photography exhibits in private and public galleries. In the new period of reform, although the press has not been completely unleashed, literature is once more interesting.

Theater

I went to the theater infrequently, because I couldn't understand much of what was happening, but I was able to enjoy observing the spectators and what was happening on the stage. Theater troupes always played to capacity crowds. Vietnamese audiences are a noisy lot, with children of all ages fidgeting and darting about, candy papers crackling, fans snapping and swishing, and much consulting with one another on the merits of the performance. I was surprised to find so many people willing to tolerate the overpowering heat and humidity. The first time I went I hadn't brought a fan, so my neighbors took turns using their fans to keep me comfortable.

Ill. 105

Until the mid-1950s, people who wanted to see a theater performance went to the cities, sometimes having to travel great distances, but during the war travel was dangerous, so the government sent the theater to the spectators – soldiers, peasants, Montagnards, and workers. This policy still exists, and today classical, folk, and musical troupes bring entertainment to the provinces.

Vietnamese theater has historically been politically conscious. Almost every play illustrates victory of the just over the strong, the kind-hearted over the evil, the merciful over the cruel. All three types of traditional theater are still performed on the stage and television; they involve music, song, and dance, with the text always in verse. *Tuong* is closest to classical Chinese opera, with plots about the affairs of ancient courts or legendary heroes, but attendance at *tuong* is diminishing because the archaic language and rigid symbolism of the actor's movements are not easily understood. *Cheo*, born and developed in the North, was originally a peasant folk opera performed by travelling troupes who mimed stories of national heroes. Later *cheo* plays criticized the unfairness of feudal and colonial society.

I liked the *cheo* plays because the elaborate court costumes, the music, the clowning, and the exaggerated gestures made it easy for me understand the rather simple plots. I've been told that today *cheo* sometimes deals with contemporary themes in traditional dress and form. The third type of traditional theater, *cai luong* had its origins in the South at the beginning of the twentieth century, and mixes traditional and contemporary music, costumes, and themes. Modern prose theater was introduced during the French era, when French acting troupes came each year to perform for the European population.

Folk theater is exceedingly popular throughout the country; Hanoi has five permanent marionette and puppet troupes, including the enchanting water puppets, unquestionably the most popular form of entertainment for tourists to Vietnam. Although water puppetry was at one time known throughout Southeast Asia, Vietnam is the only country to have continued the traditional folk art form. Water puppet shows took place in paddy fields or local ponds during village festivals. Today troupes of puppeteers perform in the cities in special theaters or converted swimming pools. The performances are lively experiences, with no serious moments. Brilliantly decorated wooden puppets skim over the water or duck under it. There are fire-spitting dragons, sparkling colored snakes, elaborate giant ducks, dancing water buffalo, dancing courtesans, and legendary heroes. Rather than one long story, performances consist of a series of five- or six-minute episodes depicting comic scenes from rural life or ferocious battles, where the hero invariably defeats the villain. The performance is enthusiastically accompanied by musicians playing traditional instruments, singers, fireworks, and frantic shouts from the puppeteers.

Ill.103-104

The wooden puppets are attached to long poles held under the water and operated by a complicated system of pulleys worked by puppeteers behind a bamboo curtain, in water up to their waists. The mechanics of each type of puppet were once a carefully guarded secret of the traditional water puppet villagers. In order not to lose the tradition, the government sponsors professional troupes who train and perform throughout Vietnam. They have travelled to Europe several times in the past few years, where they played to full houses.

Music and Dance

From neolithic and bronze age times, music and dance have been incorporated into classical and folk theater. Huge drums from the bronze age are decorated with figures of dancers and musicians performing at the royal courts and in ritual ceremonies. This classical music and dance, however, was strictly forbidden to the public and has been lost to history. Independent of the court, however, popular music and dance flourished throughout Vietnam's history, and every province and ethnic group has maintained their musical traditions.

Music has always been an important aspect of Vietnamese life. Brass gongs are used in festivals, house-warming ceremonies, rain-calling rituals, weddings, births, as a dirge for the dead, and in requiem masses held at the tombs. Scores of traditional instruments are still used: the sixteen-string zither, a mono-zither, various flutes, and many types of bamboo instruments, including a xylophone which produces beautiful, mellow sounds when the musician's hands clap air into a series of hollow bamboo sticks. (Although it looked very simple when the musician clapped her hands, after a concert a half-dozen non-Vietnamese – including me – tried to play the instrument. No matter how often we tried, or how we varied our manner of clapping, we couldn't produce the slightest sound.)

Ill. 106

The French introduced Western classical music, which is studied and performed in the larger cities; but because of the association with colonialism, it has never gained wide

66 Reminiscent of contemporaneous tomb effigies common in medieval Europe, this sculpted warrior guards the eleventh-century Van Mieu Temple of Literature.

67 Many temples are dedicated to the warrior Trung sisters, who chased the Chinese from Vietnam in 41 A.D. They are depicted here in elaborate silk embroidery.

68 At the famed one-pillar pagoda in downtown Hanoi, eleventh-century wooden elements have been restored to complement the stone fabric.

69 In its spectacular hillside setting, Hoa Lu Temple honors the warrior king who founded the Dinh Dynasty.

66

67

68

69

At the annual Dong Da festival celebrating the 1789 expulsion of the Chinese, martial arts students portray driving the invaders from Hanoi.

71 Some small boats are propelled by a seated rower handling a pair of oars; others use two rowers, each with a single oar–one forward, one standing in the stern for better forward vision and control.

72 Perhaps symbolic of their nation's future that certainly includes both the West and Vietnamese traditions, this Hanoi bride chose a contemporary western gown, her maid of honor the classic *ao dai*.

73 Prized for its spiritual symbolism in many religions, incense is especially significant in Vietnamese rituals like this ceremony at Hanoi's Van Mieu temple during Tet 1989.

74 The North Gate is all that remains of Hanoi's famed city walls, razed by the French.

72

73

74

75 Scarlet and blue silks, rich brocades, and finely detailed headgear characterize the traditional court dress donned by participants in a village festival.

76 Designed by Ho Chi Minh himself to replicate the stilt houses of the mountain people with whom he lived for many years in the jungle, Ho's modest presidential home is set in the garden behind the palace in which he refused to dwell.

75

76

77 High in the country's mountains, away from the cities and the flatlanders, Vietnam's Montagnard tribes have maintained their distinctive culture.

78 With expressions ranging from delight to puzzlement, this Montagnard family group gracefully honored the author's request to photograph them.

79 Near Dien Bien Phu, these Montagnard women wear head garb and costumes typical of the region; quilted fabric provides protection in the frequently cool mountain climate.

77

78

79

80 Her simple black velvet turban marks this woman as a member of Vietnam's "upper class".

81 Among its many distinctive beauties, Hanoi enjoys a grand array of trees of every description, even in the heart of downtown.

82 Practicality subdues subtlety in the naming of streets devoted to particular goods. This teeming lane, of course, is called Meat Street.

81

82

83 To the accompaniment of both Western instruments and traditional Vietnamese drums, this young festival performer executes a fan dance.

84 Providing both shielding from the sun and cooling insulation, Vietnam's famed conical woven hat is seen in fields and other workplaces all across the land.

85 To mask the unsightly stains caused by chewing betel nuts, the cosmetic procedure of capping women's teeth in black enamel arose, a process requiring three days.

Young women no longer follow this custom.

86 No proper traditional Vietnamese funeral procession is complete without the clangor of drums and gongs.

87 Funeral fresh flower wreaths are inevitably fashioned in an oval shape.

88 With many of its members wearing white, the color of mourning, a country funeral procession walks to the grave site.

86

87

89 Women, such as this nun
lighting incense at a pagoda
altar, play an integral role in
Buddhist life.

90 While much temple art displays highly stylized representation, some pieces convey intense emotion, such as this enameled statue in the Thay Phuong Pagoda.

91 Among the country's most powerful religious practices is the veneration of ancestors. This pagoda altar is arrayed with photographs honoring recently dead family members.

92 At prayer in a Buddhist pagoda, a nun is surrounded by silken trappings and enameled wooden statues.

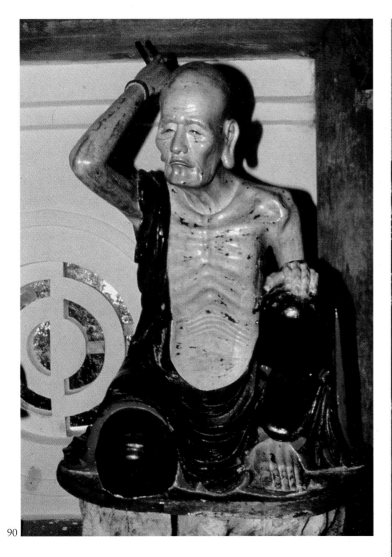

90

91

92

On a cool, overcast
morning, a vendor of
carefully arranged fresh
vegetables awaits her next
customer.

94 In villages and towns all across the land, high swings are made of bamboo for Tet. At Hanoi's Dong Da festival, a happy throng urges young men to swing higher, higher!

95 Exploration of life's mysteries is not confined to the formal temple rituals. Fortune tellers often practice their art in pagoda courtyards.

96 Perhaps not so universal as firecrackers, balloons nonetheless appear everywhere as Tet nears.

94

95

97 Returning from a bike trip of several miles to the flower villages on northern edge of Hanoi, a young woman proudly displays the fine peach blossom branch she chose to grace her home for Tet.

98 Dragon dances are sure crowd pleasers, and this one at the Dong Da Festival in Hanoi is no exception.

99 A pagoda renovation ceremony is marked by a stately procession of silk-clad, incense-bearing celebrants.

100 In addition to annual festivals, any suitable special event is occasion for a festival. The completion of a pagoda's renovation launched this vivid display.

99

100

101 When a specially notable
pagoda, such as this one
in Hanoi, is rededicated, a
grand procession opens
the celebration.

02 Enroute to Phat Diem with embassy friends, the author came accidentally upon this festival honoring the 100th year of a village pagoda some three hours southwest of Hanoi.

103 Dragons dip under the water and come up spouting fireworks during a performance by Vietnam's justly-renowned water puppeteers.

104 Even commonplace material acquires drama and charm when enacted by elaborately carved and painted water puppets.

102

103

104

This troupe performing in a
pagoda courtyard clearly
knows its business,
capturing the audience
with the theater's
irresistible magic.

106 Among Vietnam's varied
traditional musical
instruments, several are
fashioned from bamboo
for both percussion and
wind.

107 Among Vietnam's diverse
national treasures are stone
sculptures adorning
pagodas across the land,
like this fine bearded

dragon at Co Loa, near
Hanoi.

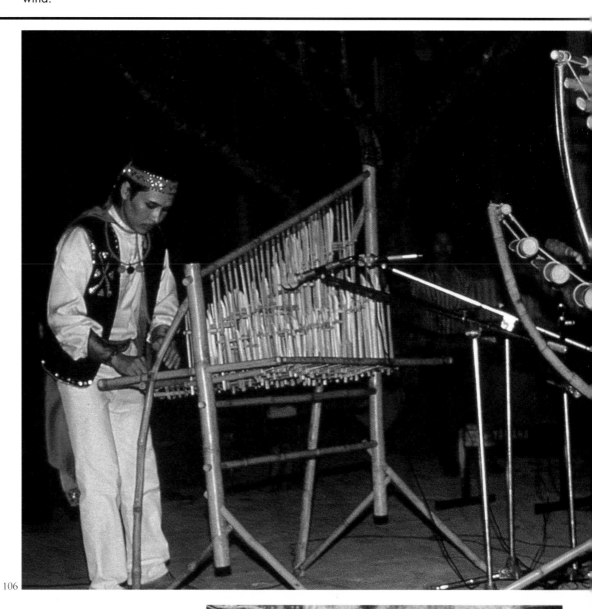

106

107

108 A professional troupe performs Montagnard dances for visiting diplomats at Hanoi's Foreign Ministry guest house.

109 Temple art works often include pieces fashioned in enameled wood, such as this statue of Quang Am at Hanoi's Vu Thach pagoda.

108

109

110 Any free moment becomes an opportunity to catch up on his English practice for this studious cyclo driver who awaits his next fare.

111 Like their counterparts in many Asian cities, these Hanoians near downtown Hoan Kiem Lake enjoy *t'ai chi* exercises at dawn.

112 With a flair of ferocity young Vietnamese athletes delight in a local variant of volleyball played with a small shuttlecock and the player's feet.

110

111

112

113 Surely not unrelated to the French legacy is the Vietnamese delight in bicycle racing. Competitors in this event cross the finish line at downtown Hanoi's Hoan Kiem Lake.

114 Members of The Red Scarf
Teenagers Organization
attend an award
Ceremony in the garden of
the Foreign Ministry
Reception building.

115 Pham Thinh directs the
international department of
the Vietnamese News
Agency, Vietnam's single
wire news service.

116 Hanoi's sanitation is poor,
with open sewers serving
many parts of the city.

117 Living conditions are
crowded, street
maintenance uneven, and
the tropical climate
mercilessly ages new
buildings in a few short

114

115

years; but city people go
about their business with
remarkably consistent
good cheer.

Because there are no
elevators, typical suburban
Hanoi concrete apartment
blocks never rise above
five stories. Although there
is indoor plumbing, water
pressure seldom functions
above the second floor.

119 Students and their teachers and administrators gather in the courtyard to inaugurate a newly-built elementary school building in Hanoi.

120 Like their counterparts in other colonial enterprises, the French in Indochina sought to recreate the trappings of their home culture. One result was buildings like this school of ballet and music in Hanoi.

121 Ranked by historians among the best strategists and tacticians of modern times, and esteemed as a national hero by his countrymen, General Giap

119

120

talks with a British
television team in the
garden of Hanoi's Foreign
Ministry Reception
building.

122 The commercial districts of Western cities are chocked with fumes and the din of countless trucks; in Hanoi the wheels of commerce are largely turned by men and women using only their own strength and determination.

123 Cyclos and bicycles are the principal mode of transport for goods and passengers.

122

123

124

24 Cyclos like this carried up to 450 pounds of supplies and dismantled artillery through the mountains to troops at Dien Bien Phu. The driver walks alongside, balancing his load with the wooden pole while steering with the handlebar.

125 Fitted with a recycled truck axle and pneumatic tires, this bullock cart is a typical example of heavy transport in town and countryside.

126 Peering through his artfully
balanced load—a living-
room suite of furniture—a
cyclo driver navigates a
rain-washed Hanoi street.

127 Rice plants are commonly irrigated by shifting canal water into paddies using roped baskets deftly swung between two workers.

128 Like nearly every industry in the country, lumbering thrives despite the lack of machinery. Planks are generally sawn by two-man teams in small workshops.

129 Because there is virtually no agricultural machinery, farmers rely on traditional garden tools.

127

128

130 Excavation of an apartment building foundation proceeds, like every phase of construction, with only simple hand tools.

131 Hoes and cultivators are principal agricultural tools throughout the land.

132 In hand-making bricks, clay is pressed individually into wooden molds.

130

131

132

Clay for bricks vital to new
construction is dug by
hand from pits outside
Hanoi.

134 Stopping to allow her passengers to swim along sandy beaches, this tourist boat plods among Ha Long Bay's thousands of limestone islets.

135 Dr. Nguyen Li Trang works with an assistant at Hanoi's Institute for Hygiene and Epidemiology.

136 His shop cat snoozes while the portrait artist in his sidewalk studio attempts to generate the day's next subject.

137 The author's son, Timothy Gift, found that Western tourists were rare enough to stir a curious welcome from village children.

134

135

136

137

popularity. A few Vietnamese musicians enter international competitions and participate in organizations, such as The Chopin Society. At several small concerts I attended I couldn't fail to notice the woefully tattered sheet music; pages looked as though they might fall apart if turned one more time. It was also touching to see the pressed and clean threadbare black tuxedos, shirts and black bow ties of the men – clothing not sold in Vietnam since colonial times.

In spite of feudal and colonial attempts to restrict expression of Vietnamese cultural traditions, folk dances have always been popular, and remain so. Vietnamese choreography is characterized by lightness and grace, and does not involve acrobatics. Hand gestures prevail over footwork, and dancers frequently employ such accessories as hats, kerchiefs, fans, and small bells; feet generally simply mark the rhythm. The dances themselves often relate simple folk tales or love stories; some mimic rural activities.

Ill. 108

Art

The beginnings of Vietnam's artistic heritage are illustrated in the drawings and carvings on cave walls in Dong Noi, near Hanoi, and on objects crafted of bone, shell, and ceramics. Later drawings from the bronze age exhibit a refined and light-hearted combination of realism and stylization that includes geometric patterns, flocks of deer and aquatic birds, and human figures playing musical instruments, dancing, or performing manual labor. Men are clad in feather garments, giving them an aspect of bird-men and call to mind Mayan and Aztec images. During the Chinese occupation, from 111 B.C. to A.D. 927, the Dong Son (Bronze Period) pattern of decoration went underground, not to be seen again until it was noticed in contemporary fabrics woven by Montagnard women.

Ill.. 107

Art from the Chinese era survives primarily in funerary sculpture, in addition to a wide variety of ceramic wares. Following the expulsion of the Chinese in the tenth century, Vietnamese art became essentially Buddhist art.

Decoration on the pagodas and temples today seems to continue that described by early historians and travelers. Elaborately carved and painted columns, beams, and altars, each with scores of lacquer-painted wooden sculptures, range in size from six inches to twenty feet. In the humblest of pagodas and temples may be found dozens of statues of Buddha, arhats (servants of Buddha), legendary kings, warrior heroes, and sometimes Confucius and Lao Tsu (the founder of Taoism). A favorite is Quan Am, the goddess of mercy and guardian of children, frequently depicted sitting on a lotus flower; at other times she stands, dressed in a long white robe with a scarf draped over her head, looking very much like the Virgin Mary.

Ill. 109

While most remaining Cham art is located in the country's south central region, some stone statues were brought to the North by armies returning from their conquest of the Champa empire in 1471 (there's a fine one at Hoa Lu). The Cham's intricately carved stone towers and sculptures are reminiscent of their Hindu origins.

Lacking the durability of stone, few paintings survive from traditional times. The brutally destructive Ming occupation from 1406 to 1428 and Hanoi's repeated sackings further reduced the number of early paintings, principally landscapes, battle scenes, and portraits of kings and heroes. Many, created for religious purposes and executed on wood panels, reflect themes from Buddha's life or scenes of the underworld.

North of Hanoi, the artisans of Dong Ho village have been making their distinctive, rather primitive wood block prints since the sixteenth century. The popular prints are hung over ancestral altars during Tet and can be found in the markets at festivals and on small stands that pop up during the New Year season. They are most prized in rural areas, where people love them because they reflect their daily life, their social, and even political opinions. Revolutionary art, most frequently woodblock posters, proliferated when artists were called upon to help educate and rouse the populace during the fight against colonialism. The posters are not much to my taste, but after seeing so many during my stay, a few of them began to appeal to me; I finally bought several, including one showing the Trung sisters going off to war on their elephants. Mind you, they are still sitting on a shelf, not on my walls. They are perhaps among those art forms that seem a good idea when you discover them as a tourist but, like some wines and cheeses, don't travel well.

Today's artists exhibit paintings in state museums, shops, and private galleries. Since 1987 the number of private galleries, located in people's homes where a cup of tea is usually offered to visitors, has been steadily increasing. I regularly visited a number of state stores and private galleries and, because the prices were so reasonable, I brought home a number of lovely paintings.

Contemporary oil painting, using techniques introduced during the French era, appears heavily derivative of early twentieth-century Western art, and not, to my eye, particularly interesting; the examples I saw seemed out of place in Vietnam. Far more attractive, I found, are paintings on silk, much the most popular medium among today's Vietnamese artists, and particularly suitable for Oriental landscapes and those morning and evening seascapes when the light refracts through mist. Occasionally, interesting woodblock prints and metal etchings turn up. Current artists generally favor conventional and non-controversial material, such as pastoral scenes with young women in *ao dais*, traditional festival scenes, heroes on elephants, village and city street scenes, village markets peopled with peasants in pre-colonial costumes, still-lifes, and not a few nudes. The occasional non-figurative painter notwithstanding, abstraction is not much in evidence.

Many experts consider Vietnamese lacquer painting, a medium dating from fifteenth-century China, to be the finest in the world, highly prized in Europe as well as in the East. Black, red, and a yellowish-brown are the principal colors, and many layers of glossy clear lacquer create an illusion of great depth. Vietnam is the only country where the traditional eggshell and oil technique is still practiced; fragile dots of eggshell are worked into the lacquer, sometimes augmented by gold or silver dust, creating an unusual, shimmering effect.

Among lacquer techniques for decorating functional objects, relief work and mother-of-pearl inlay allow dramatic effects. In relief paintings, a design is cut into the many-layered lacquer and painted in various colors, giving a glossy effect and an impression of depth. In the mother-of-pearl procedure, mosaic-like images are created by fitting precisely chiseled bits of the iridescent shell into lacquered wood.

Lacquer is the preferred decoration for cult objects in temples and pagodas: statues, trays, drums, altars, vases, incense burners, and the wooden columns, doorways, and beams of the building itself. The predominant color is a brownish dark red, which creates a warm, rich atmosphere in the reflections of candle and lamplight.

During the wars, sculptors were not in demand, so a hiatus in training and inspiration occurred. After 1954, with the need for war memorials, realistic sculpture appeared, mostly in the socialist realism style typical of Communist countries, work which must surely jar the sensibilities of a people accustomed to more refined art. Remarking on these memorial sculptures, a prominent Vietnamese art critic noted: "Their number is quite high, but their quality is still low."

Contemporary crafts include ceramics, lacquerware, embroidery on silk and cotton, lacework, bamboo and rattan furniture, and functional articles such as baskets, bags, trays, lamp shades. Decorative motifs run to lotus flowers, dragons, phoenixes, and portraits. Lacework, introduced by the French, includes fine crocheted tablecloths, curtains, and clothing.

Literature

Reading material remains extremely scarce in Vietnam, a particular hardship in a country with a literacy rate above some Western countries. As with most of Vietnam's problems, the reason is economic and technological: a long-term serious shortage of paper. As a result, books are a precious commodity. Imported books in English are not quite worth their weight in gold, but from the reactions of Vietnamese suddenly in possession of one, it would seem so. Those who can afford the luxury build small personal libraries by photocopying books and articles at the new photocopy shops.

The first time I lent a hard cover book to a Vietnamese English teacher in my class, he looked at it in astonishment, held the volume carefully in one hand while he caressed the cover and inside pages with the other. Saying to me, "This is the first time I've seen a book with a hard cover," he called out to several colleagues and students across the courtyard. They gathered around us to admire the smooth texture and whiteness of the pages, so marked a contrast to Vietnamese books printed on coarse, beige paper. Watching these teachers and students react with such delight to my book was one more reminder of how spoiled we are in the West. When I asked one of my embassy contacts to bring in a sampling of the slick and glossy magazines we take for much so granted in the West, my Hanoi colleagues were awed, their minds blown away.

Everyone reads. Cyclo drivers read while waiting for customers, people squat on the sidewalks with a book in hand, market women read between serving customers, merchants sit in doorways and ignore browsing potential clients. Many times I saw passengers on the backs of bicycles calmly reading while being pedaled through the most hazardous traffic imaginable. Reading is an important part of Vietnamese life.

Ill. 110

Until the twentieth century, when French became the country's second language, two separate literatures thrived in Vietnam: *han*, the classical literary Chinese used for philosophical and historical works and scholarly poetry, and *nom* Vietnamese, for stories, tales, and poems of popular inspiration. In the seventeenth century Jesuit priests devised a Roman alphabet for *nom*, which is still in use. Dispensing with the thousands of ideographs made it much easier to learn to read and write, and may be one of the reasons why Vietnam's is among the highest literacy rates in the world.

The earliest remaining Vietnamese literature, written by Buddhist monks in both poetry and prose, dates from the tenth and eleventh centuries. Religious and nationalistic works encouraged people to struggle for national survival; later writings criticized decadent dynastic regimes, or praised nature and the simple life. This popular literature was severely censored and repressed by the emperors, but the verse stories were too popular to eliminate entirely.

During the eighteenth century the popular work of three famous women poets – Doan Thi Diem, Ho Xuan Huong, and Thanh Quan – severely criticized their male-dominated, feudal society with a refined sarcasm and humor that would undoubtedly be appreciated by today's Western feminists.

In traditional times poetry was esteemed far above prose, and contemporary Vietnamese continue to cherish their poetry, most particularly in the North. It is not unusual to see couples sitting on the sidewalk reading poems to each other. During the war, nearly every northern soldier carried a small notebook in which he wrote his thoughts in poetic form. Army officials at one time decided that too much time was being spent on such writing: their directive against diaries was generally ignored. An overseas Vietnamese tourist in Hanoi told me delightedly about one cyclo driver who composed a "very good" poem for her as he pedaled to her destination.

According to Stan Reedy, an aid administrator studying Vietnamese in Hanoi, the country's love for poetry has a practical benefit for foreigners studying the language: "It isn't very difficult to be a beginner; the grammar is simple, and if you mix up your syntax, the

Vietnamese merely think you're being poetical."

Interest in literature is reflected in the many literary reviews and journals that enjoy wide circulation. The Communist Party-controlled publishing houses favor works illustrating the heroism and sacrifice of the war years, but recent reforms permit publication of authors who take a realistic look at post-war Vietnamese society.

Foreign literature has never been censored and, officially, anyone can read whatever books, periodicals, or newspapers he or she can lay hands on, but several times I noted that when I gave a Vietnamese friend an old newsmagazine, it was quickly tucked out of sight. English language magazines and newspapers are not sold in Vietnam; the Vietnamese could never afford them. One foreign language publishing house prints original language and translations of foreign literature, but the director told me their budget is so low, and paper so scarce, that they print only several per year.

Film

Vietnamese cinema had its birth in 1945, with a newsreel of Ho Chi Minh's proclamation of Vietnam's independence. Early films recorded major battles, such as Dien Bien Phu, evidence of American bombing, or were "inspirational," to encourage war production. Documentaries aimed at strengthening the war economy by educating peasants how to produce better crops, and training films helped to educate the militia and civilian air defence. In addition to newsreels and documentaries, some films used animated drawings and puppets.

U.S. bombing drove the projection of movies under ground, literally, when films were shown to people in their subterranean meeting rooms. To entertain soldiers and workers, six hundred mobile teams carried projectors and films around the country by truck, boat, and on foot. In combat areas, projection was managed with hand-operated projectors, acetylene lamps, and small gasoline-powered electric generators.

Until very recently, non-documentary movies were limited to stories of revolutionary heroism on the battlefield or the tractor front and upbeat themes depicting the "wonderful post-war socialist life." Now filmmakers are permitted to deal with realistic subjects that would have been unacceptable several years ago. One frank documentary by Tran Van Thuy vividly contrasts the lives of Vietnam's contemporary "haves" and "have-nots." Such films assessing social and political values are allowed, but may bring their makers difficulties if they criticize the Party too strongly.

But the Vietnamese love the movies, and because there aren't enough Vietnamese films to satisfy the market, many are imported, mostly from Communist countries. Dubbing and sub-titles are too expensive, so a translator sits off-stage with a microphone and simultaneously translates. (The use of a translator to interpret the story surprised me when I went to see the ballet *Spartacus*.)

As in every discipline, the Vietnamese make do with antiquated and make-shift equipment and technology. I was taken to visit a film studio, which consisted of a few dilapidated office and storage buildings. The sound stage was an old hangar once used by French seaplanes operating from the West Lake. Only catwalks had been added. The camera equipment looked to me as if it should be in a museum. But, despite all these handicaps, a few Vietnamese films have earned critical acclaim on recent tours through the United States and Europe. Vietnam's version of Hollywood's Oscars, the Golden Lotuses, are presented to prizewinning films at a biennial film festival.

Pirate videos from Bangkok and Hong Kong are shown in small, impromptu theaters, private homes, or in restaurants, where admission is charged. Judging by the posters I saw, there seems to be a preference for violent, martial arts epics. But it could be that these films are simply the most easily accessible.

Radio and Television

Although the Vietnamese media is controlled and censored by the government, people are free to listen to the Voice of America and BBC radio broadcasts and uncensored Soviet satellite television transmissions.

The country's only radio station, the Voice of Vietnam, was launched in September 1945, when it broadcast Ho Chi Minh's Declaration of Independence on a small transmitter left behind by the French. Throughout the French war, from 1946 to 1954, the service broadcast from Ho's headquarters in the jungles of Viet Bac, purportedly without a day's interruption. In 1954 the operation was moved to Hanoi where, according to records, it lost only nine minutes of transmission time throughout all the years of American bombing.

In addition to some thirteen hours of domestic broadcasting each day, the Voice of Vietnam transmits more than twenty-five hours weekly of programming in twelve foreign languages. These programs include Vietnamese news, music, and feature stories on Vietnamese history or culture.

I worked several hours a week as a volunteer in the English division, editing articles translated by the six-member staff, primarily from the Party newspaper, before they were given to the news announcers. I was surprised to see scores of letters received weekly from listeners throughout the world, including the American Midwest.

Ownership of television sets has mushroomed in the past few years. Until recently, sets could only be purchased in state stores at prices few could afford, but with the changing economy and imports of electronic goods from Japan, they have now become more readily available. VCR players have opened a new cultural vista for the middle class and are an undeniable token of affluence. Extended families pool their savings until they accumulate enough to buy a set. It is common to see a boxed TV headed for home on the back rack of someone's bicycle or motorbike.

For five to six hours each day two channels transmit a mix of news, language training, interviews, movies, and traditional or modern music and dance, and once a week a program of traditional theater.

Sports

The government has always encouraged exercise as a means of staying healthy. Because the lack of medicines and medical technology makes life particularly precarious for older people, many belong to "Golden Age" clubs that, among other activities, organize daily *tai chi* sessions. During early mornings, groups in the parks may be seen going through the slow-motion, ballet-like exercises. *Tai chi* appears simple but, after taking lessons, I soon learned that it is both intellectually and physically exacting. I wasn't very adept, but I did come to better appreciate the art when watching Hanoians on my dawn excursions around the city.   Ill. 111

Competing with the *tai chi* practitioners for park or sidewalk space at daybreak were the badminton players. People of all ages play, with or without nets, for half an hour or more before going to work. I used to enjoy being awakened by the shouts of delight following successful shots, or grunts over missed birds during the games underway in the park across the street from my room.

The most popular team sports are soccer and volleyball, but children are rarely seen playing these games because balls are expensive. A form of volleyball is played on the sidewalks and in the parks by boys and young men – never girls or women; instead of a ball they use homemade shuttlecocks which they kick with their heels. Real nets are seldom seen; participants use an imaginary net or improvise one with parked bicycles or strung-together shirts.

Individual sports include marathon racing, the martial arts, bicycle racing, and swimming. In areas threatened with yearly floods, villages hold competitions for "Community Whose Members Know How To Swim." I met a couple who were Australian Olympic swimming trainers in Hanoi working with Vietnam's swim team helping them prepare for the next Olympics.

Ill. 112

At the national level, the General Department of Physical Education and Sports promotes the development of amateur and professional teams, and sponsors training centers. In 1989 Vietnamese athletes participated in the ASEAN (Association of Southeast Asian Nations) Games for the first time, but their performance was disappointing. The trainer attributed his team's lackluster rankings to the country's long isolation, "Because Vietnam was previously cut off from international competition, we were not aware of new techniques and tactics. We have a lot to learn."

Ill. 113

What they lack in technique, they frequently make up in stamina. The February 1992 issue of the *Indochina Digest* reported that in an international marathon in Ho Chi Minh City, seven of the first ten finishers were Vietnamese who could not afford sports shoes and ran barefoot in 90° heat.

Cuisine

Having spent many a wonderful evening in the many Vietnamese restaurants in Paris, I was prepared to enjoy "real" Vietnamese food. And I did. My favorite discovery was *pho,* the Northern specialty noodle soup, which I could happily eat for breakfast, lunch, and dinner – though not all on the same day.

The Vietnamese take pride in their cuisine, eaten with chopsticks, and invariably present it attractively, no matter how humble the fare. When sufficient ingredients are available, the cuisine is refined and delicious. Unfortunately, most Vietnamese must make do with below-standard rations.

Because of cramped living conditions and primitive kitchen facilities, many Vietnamese eat at small, inexpensive sidewalk restaurants. I was lured to many of these "establishments" (often a few square feet of sidewalk with miniature stools and tables) when I wasn't even hungry, because of the wonderful smells from the *pho* vats and good things cooking on charcoal braziers. Since the lifting of restrictions on private enterprise, larger restaurants located in one or two rooms of private homes spring up almost weekly. Walking through or past the kitchens does not inspire confidence, but the food served is delicious by any standards. I found the tourist hotels' food lackluster but adequate.

Governing

"Waging war is simple, but running a country is very difficult."
Pham Van Dong, Prime Minster for more than thirty years

Knowing that Vietnam's government was totalitarian, I was prepared for an abundance of armed police, as I've seen in my travels to other authoritarian states, right and left. But during the nearly two years I lived there, I saw armed policemen only in front of a few embassies and at the Foreign Ministry guest house where foreign dignitaries stay, none at the airport or government buildings and never in the streets. Uniformed policemen were on duty in the city, but not so many as in an average American city. Hanoi's policemen were often smiling and extremely laid back. Pedestrians would stop to gossip and laugh with them, sometimes slapping them on the back to emphasize a point in the conversation. Traffic police attempted to produce some sort of order out of the chaos they were presented with daily, but just shrugged their shoulders when someone did something that in most countries would earn them a stiff fine.

The first time I saw street vendors excitedly gather up their wares and scurry in the opposite direction from an approaching policeman, I was afraid they would be arrested. Rather than taking off for distant parts, the curbside entrepreneurs simply dashed around the nearest corner and stuck their heads out from behind the building, laughing. As soon as the policeman had gone on his way, back they came to their spots to set up business again. I thought to myself, "These are not a fearful people."

The average citizen is careful not to do obvious things that would annoy the Party, such as spending too much private time with foreigners or writing letters to the editor advocating a free press and multiple political parties. But, as many Vietnamese explained to me, they do not fear the knock on the door in the night or other such police state intimidation. Their greatest concern seems to be the possibility of losing an opportunity for promotion if there are negative notes in their dossiers.

Communist Party members fill all key government positions. The party maintains exclusivity by its invitation-only membership, now about 1.8 million – less than three percent of the population. A network of party cadres leads the many mass organizations, such the Ho Chi Minh Communist Youth League, the Women's Union, the Red Scarf Teenager's Organization, and the Fatherland Front, which unites a number of subordinate groups. Ill. 114

Although many Vietnamese openly express disgust about the failure of Communist leadership to control the economy, the fierce hatred of the Party common in other Communist countries is not evident. Party loyalty is greatest amongst older people, who fought the wars and who are reluctant to accept the evidence that those responsible for winning the wars seem unable to find a way to run the country. There is growing concern among Party officials over a decline in new memberships. *Nhan Dan*, the Party paper, reported a study showing only 15% of young people in the industrial sector plan to join the Party, down from 30% before the fall of Communism in the Eastern Bloc countries.

Many younger people have long been disillusioned with the Party and are pessimistic about its ability to solve today's problems: "They've been in the tunnels too long."

Institutions

Vietnam's head of state is the prime minister, who is also the Secretary of the Communist Party, but he is no dictator. The country is ruled by consensus of the Politburo of the Party and a two-chamber legislature – the National Assembly, and a fifteen-member Council of State appointed by the Assembly – a method of governance that has proven to be cumbersome and inefficient.

The National Assembly is a representative body of 496 members (elected every five years) who need not be Communist Party members; in 1990 nearly two-thirds were not. The new era of reform has somewhat strengthened the Assembly, which used to be a rubber-stamp for the Party. In 1989 the Assembly began openly to debate government policy, such as strictures on freedom of the press, and once held up approval of the national budget by firing tough questions at ministers about how they were running their departments.

A three-year stint in the army is compulsory for men between the ages of 18 and 27. Women may enlist only if they belong to the Ho Chi Minh Youth League. The army is not militaristic in the sense in which the term is understood in the West. There is no military-industrial complex; no one benefits from military-related investments. One Vietnamese general told me, "Soldiers are seen as servants of the people." That notion is realized in practice. Military units serve the country in various independent economic ventures, such as running large state farms and coal mines, building roads and bridges, operating garages and commercial fisheries and other enterprises.

Vietnam has never experienced anything remotely like a China-style Cultural Revolution. The several experts with whom I spoke do not believe such an upheaval possible, even in the furthest imaginative leap, any more than they could envision the sort of upheaval or repression that bloodied Beijing's Tienanmen Square in 1989. As a non-expert, I agree.

Since 1987 the state has moved to make the press more assertive and responsible to the public, and for a while the government encouraged reporters to "search out the negative elements" of society. Stories appeared attacking corruption in high places and, according to the editor of *Nhan Dan*, the Party paper, the Party was purged of more than 100,000 members in the late 1980s. But, compared to the West, the new Vietnamese muckraking is exceedingly bland stuff. Party leader Nguyen Van Linh recently reminded the press that it has not been unleashed to do whatever it wishes. "The press must reflect the voice of the people, but it must first of all be a tool of the Party, to speak the voice of the Party . . . explain the Party's and [the] State's correct views to the people, and help them better understand the Party's policies and the State's laws . . . The press is the mouthpiece of the Party."

The result, of course, is that the newspapers are crashingly boring, a fact not lost on the Vietnamese. My Foreign Ministry class had asked me to talk about the press in America, which I did, to their great fascination. All had believed that the American government financed the press, how else could papers be printed? When I explained advertising and the profit motive, they seemed to begin to comprehend how the press could be independent of the government. In the interest of exposing my students to as many different types of accents and speaking styles as possible, I invited visiting Americans to speak to my classes. When Clay Jones of the *Christian Science Monitor* came to speak, my students probed him closely, and they seemed satisfied that he confirmed what I had already told them about the press. That this class of Foreign Ministry students felt free enough to publicly pose the questions they did suggested to me a certain tolerance on the part of the Party/Government, since class activities were monitored.

On my last class day, the students queried me about my impressions of life in Vietnam. In most of my replies, I could be totally candid without fear of hurting anyone's feelings. However, when one fellow asked what I thought of Vietnamese newspapers, I hesitated. (The group knew I was aware of the sorts of things printed, since their assignments often included translations of news articles into English, which we compared and went over in class – in part, my sneaky way of learning all that I could about what was happening in the country.) I suggested that none of the papers would last three days in an American city. When asked why, I finally said, "Because they're boring!" Almost everyone in the class broke into smiles and said they agreed with me.

Monumental bureaucratic inefficiency is another wonder of Vietnamese life, but hardly a propitious one. Some observers blame the creaking jumble of inertia and redundancy in part on the French who, unlike their British counterparts in India, failed to develop an administrative structure and cadre among the indigenous people. Nothing like the immensely competent Indian Civil Service graced Saigon or Hanoi when the French departed. Upon an unprepared population were thrust the responsibilities of government at a time when the country's most able men and women were totally occupied with an epochal military struggle. When peace finally came, Vietnam's government tackled the nation's staggering administrative problems with no more sophisticated tools than Communism's notoriously ponderous central planning apparatus.

In an effort to keep unemployment figures low and to reward loyal Party members, ministries are hugely overstaffed with people who do nothing except try to appear essential by delaying papers that need a stamp or signature, and nothing can be done with only one signature or stamp. In many cases, ignorant and arrogant officials hold positions of power only because of Party loyalties. Without exception, foreign aid workers express disgust with "the system", but put up with it "because the Vietnamese people deserve to be helped." Communication between ministries is cumbersome and often sabotaged by bureaucratic jealousies; decisions are put off until the last moment or simply ignored. Millions of dollars of allocated international aid money go unspent, for example, because no one makes the decisions needed to implement the projects.

This being said, many talented and dedicated officials in Vietnam well appreciate the problems and have spearheaded efforts to coordinate and streamline their ministries. And at the front line of dealing with the public, the civil servants manning the windows usually do their best to serve and accommodate, no matter how inefficient the process.

Party leaders, keenly aware of events in other Communist countries, are seeking to make the Party and government more responsive to the people by giving more autonomy to local authorities. Beneath the surface of open debate, powerful currents for multi-party democracy are fast eroding the Party's base of support, but hard-liners, repelled by the idea of political change, still wield enormous power. Others realize that the Party's fortunes are tied to results of its economic reforms which encourage free enterprise; they recognize that such success will inevitably intensify demands for political democracy.

Housing

Adequate urban housing has been one of the government's most elusive goals. The enormous need created by the destruction of an estimated 80,000 urban homes during the war was aggravated as peasants made their way to the cities when their villages were destroyed. Others headed to the cities in search of employment.

According to government figures, more than half of present urban housing does not meet minimum standards. As late as 1987, the average amount of living space nationwide amounted to some 46 square feet per person. Southern cities average a bit more – 55 square feet.

Northern urban areas average 35 square feet, but Hanoi, a scant 24 square feet.

Private ownership of housing nationwide is forty-two percent (though higher in the South.) Most private homes are one story high, of hand-made brick covered with a layer of concrete, frequently painted a pastel color, with roofs of hand-made terra cotta tiles. (The construction date is traditionally marked in large numerals somewhere above the door). Even in new housing, amenities are scarce: windows have no glass, only bars and wooden shutters, nor is there central heating or even fireplaces to combat the frequently bitter cold of the northern winters.

Water supply and sewage systems are strained to the limit in the cities. According to a recent survey, in urban areas only one in five units has running water, and public faucets and fountains are shared by an average of 900 people. Where it is not piped, water is obtained from shallow wells (usually unprotected and therefore polluted), rainwater collection tanks, streams, and ponds. Sanitary facilities are marginal as well: in Hanoi an average of thirty persons share a toilet, say government figures, and in workers' districts that figure can rise to one hundred.

Private contractors have been discouraged from entering the housing market because of rent controls and the difficulty in repossessing housing if renters default. The lack of money and modern technology hinder progress; apartment blocks continue to be largely built by manual labor using handmade bricks and bamboo scaffolding.

Health Care

People in Vietnam die from diseases that are preventable in almost any other country, where vaccines, medicines, and preventive care are accessible. The biggest killers are tuberculosis, malaria, cholera, bubonic plague, Japanese encephalitis, diarrheal diseases, polio, leprosy, and acute respiratory infections – many aggravated by smoking. (Almost every adult Vietnamese male smokes.)

Although a recent survey by the UNDP found that the nation's health care structure and trained public health personnel are superior than those in most other developing countries – and even superior to some countries in the lower middle income group – it is, nevertheless, impossible to receive quality health care in Vietnam. There simply is not enough equipment or medicine, partly the result of the U.S.-led embargo. Hospital patients lie three to a double bed, and must supply their own clothing and food. Severe shortages of vaccines and essential drugs, such as antibiotics, hamper disease prevention and treatment. Equipment stands rusting for lack of spare parts or maintenance; wheelchairs tilt and sag, wheels bent, seats torn; in operating rooms gritty dust drifts in through broken windows, doors won't close, and lamps hang dark over operating tables, with no spare bulbs to be had. One evening I met a first-time visitor to Vietnam who had just toured Hanoi's best hospital. She was weeping when she said, "It's like visiting something from the Middle Ages."

There are neither enough textbooks and other medical learning materials, nor training facilities for maintenance technicians. When I first arrived in Hanoi and inquired of the diplomatic community about health care for myself, I was told, "If any Westerner gets anything more serious than a hangnail, he gets on the plane to Bangkok." A World Health Organization (WHO) representative told me, "Vietnam has every disease known to man. You can tell when the plague comes up from the South because of all the dead rats in the streets." (Whenever I saw a dead rat in the street thereafter, I slowed down to study it carefully, to determine if it had been run over or had expired before reaching its destination.)

Visiting Western medical workers are appalled by the pitiful resources with which the medical professionals in Vietnam must work, and are amazed at what is accomplished with so little. On seeing a small clothesline strung with surgical gloves and strands of bandages that had been re-washed to the point of near disintegration, a visiting American urologist sadly observed, "Any Vietnamese hospital could exist for a year on what my hospital throws away in a week."

The UNDP concluded that although there is an adequate supply of trained health personnel (before World War II there was one physician for each 180,000 people, today the figures are one for every 3,076, and one medical graduate or assistant doctor for each 960), without technical resources and medicines, little can to be done to improve the level of health care delivery.

Because Western medical supplies and pharmaceuticals are unavailable, traditional medicine, including acupuncture, has remained an important part of health care. The government encourages people to share their family household remedies, and offers cash rewards to those who give their formulas to health authorities for dissemination throughout the country. The donor receives a share of profits from sales or may manufacture the medicine himself. Some of the ingredients from home recipes sound exotic, such as one that calls for "bitter dragon skin," which, on investigation, turns out to be the popular name for the bark of a particular variety of tree.

Sanitation remains a serious problem in both rural and urban areas. Inadequate sewage disposal and contaminated water pose ongoing health hazards, and insufficient preventive care remains responsible for the high disease rate and lack of good health generally. Dental care is woefully inadequate. It is estimated that fewer than five percent of Vietnamese children possess toothbrushes, while most of them have cavities and periodontal disease.

To cope with the war's legacy of tens of thousands of disabled people, a special ministry was created. Government sources report that an estimated thirteen percent of the population is disabled as a result of war, accidents, or congenital deformities, including those resulting from Agent Orange, the defoliant widely used by the U.S. military during the war. Mobile health teams, including specialists in physiotherapy and orthopedics, serve in the rural areas, but a drastic shortage of materials for making prostheses means that very few of those without limbs can be helped. Underequipped rehabilitation centers are scattered throughout the country, all suffering a plague of shortages.

Mental health care combines Western and traditional therapies and acupuncture; emphasis is on at-home care because there are not nearly enough hospital beds. Consulting rooms at district and village levels are able to care for only 120,000 of the estimated 650,000 who need mental help.

With monthly salaries averaging twelve to twenty dollars, doctors and other health personnel, like nearly everyone else in the country, must work outside their regular eight-hour, six-day week to earn enough to live on. Most doctors hold consultations in their homes at night or work double shifts at their hospital. Others work nights as cyclo drivers; both men and women tailor clothes at home, work as translators, roll cigarettes, or work at any other menial occupation they can find. Many hospitals permit doctors and nurses to cook in their hospital canteens that double as public restaurants.

Education

One of Ho Chi Minh's first acts after declaring Vietnam's independence was to initiate a literacy campaign. "Everyone of you must know his rights and duties. He must possess knowledge so as to be able to participate in the building of the country . . . let the literates teach the illiterates, let the illiterates study hard." The crusade continued into the French war with itinerant teachers following their students around the country, teaching them to read between battles. At independence, literacy was estimated at five to ten percent. After three concentrated programs lasting until 1954, the rate had climbed to an estimated eighty to ninety percent in the North. After reunification in 1975 another, equally successful, literacy campaign was initiated in the South, where education of the peasants had been largely neglected by Diem and later regimes.

Education today, however, is precarious. Classroom conditions range from dreary to appalling. Paint is a luxury, and little can be spared for schools; there are no such niceties as charts, maps, or illustrations for the walls; planks of wood, sometimes with a coat of green paint, serve as chalkboards; doors don't close, electricity is frequently interrupted, and textbooks are in severely short supply. Glassless windows pose a genuine hardship when rudimentary shutters are little comfort against the North's bitter winter winds. (One winter day my classroom at the International Relations Institute was so cold I was unable to hold chalk in my ungloved hands. My students were visibly shivering in their layered clothing. I finally dismissed class.) Open shutters also mean that dust settles on everything within seconds after cleaning. Grounds and courtyards are grassless, dusty fields. University campuses fare no better than primary and secondary schools; cheerless places, they resemble factory compounds.

Class sizes at primary through university levels average fifty students, with some as high as seventy. Schools, like offices and factories, function six days a week, and most primary and lower secondary schools operate on two or three shifts. Students bring brooms from home and take turns cleaning the school because there are no funds for janitorial help.

Children are required to complete at least nine years of school. But in order to keep up with Vietnam's dizzying 2.4 percent birthrate (1989), some experts estimate that one hundred new classrooms must be built every day. As throughout much of the world, Vietnam teachers are poorly paid. In order to survive, like everyone else, they must moonlight at second jobs. One high school teacher told me about travelling to the opposite side of town to sell cigarettes on the sidewalk because, "It is embarrasing to have one of your students come up to buy cigarettes from you."

Fortunate teachers whose subject is in demand can teach in private schools at night or tutor small groups in their homes, a practice that sometimes creates an odd catch-22. Reported an English student at Hanoi University, "I have to take lessons at a private night school because my university teacher is absent so frequently – taking time off to give private lessons for extra money – that I can't learn enough in class to pass the examinations."

In spite of poor salaries, teaching remains an honorable, even prestigious profession. On National Teacher's Day, streets are filled with people carrying bouquets of flowers for teachers. Each of the groups I taught gave me flowers and presents: a beautiful embroidered jacket, which they'd commissioned one of their members to make, a beautifully decorated French-style cake, expensive sweets, a picture book about Vietnam, and a lovely black and white carved bone necklace. It was like Christmas.

But respect doesn't put food on the table, and the profession's dismal working conditions and inadequate pay have caused today's serious shortage of teachers. Many leave the profession for more lucrative jobs in factories or small family businesses. I met a young woman selling sundries at a small street stand. When I complimented her excellent English, she told me she had been an English teacher but quit because she could make more money selling lipsticks on the sidewalk.

Public clamor about deteriorating education recently led the government to initiate school fees in order to generate funds for upgrading the schools. For the first time, students unable to pass the entrance exams may still attend government universities, but on a fee-paying basis. Also, the government recently allowed the operation of private schools and university level colleges, euphemistically called "People Funded Schools." In 1989 two precedent-setting schools opened their doors to full classes: the first private secondary school in Hanoi, and the first non-state higher education science institute, Thang Long College. The two schools' long
Ill.119-120 waiting lists raised expectations that the number of private educational institutions will increase rapidly.

Other government reform includes replacement of unqualified Party members on the administrative level with properly credentialed educators. Visiting a school one day, I asked teachers if they felt they were any better off since the coming of *doi moi* (the opening to the West and general reform). "Oh, yes," they replied, "now we have an experienced teacher for our director, and we feel there is an appreciation of our problems."

On the university level, overseas study has provided a partial solution to educational problems. Soviet universities have trained over 70,000 specialists, and other Communist bloc countries perhaps an additional 30,000. Through the late 1950s, 30,000 were trained in China. Following Communism's collapse in Europe, such training drastically decreased.

Science and Technology

Access to international scientific research came to a standstill during the wars, and Vietnam has not yet been able to catch up with the West's scientific and technological advances. Improvement has been hindered not only by the U.S. embargo, but the scarcity of funds for research; there is not even enough money for subscriptions to Western scientific journals.

The country's extensive network of scientific institutes suffers from a lack of equipment routinely found in any small American high school lab, and most of what they have is hopelessly outdated. Scientists are generally skilled and well educated, many with foreign degrees, but most are not able to work at their profession efficiently because, apart from the lack of equipment and supplies, they are forced to employ their time and laboratory equipment to earn extra money for themselves and their institutions. Some chemistry research labs make wine or beer to sell on the market, while others make incense, mosquito repellant, and other consumer items. Instead of printing maps desperately needed for development of Vietnam's infrastructure, the Cartography Institute prints calling cards, wedding invitations, and cigarette packages.

Scientific and technological progress is also hampered by the bureaucracy. Too many institutes are headed by former war heroes or loyal Party members who have no scientific qualifications, and who make uninformed and arbitrary decisions about research projects and the allocation of equipment and personnel resources. The government recently acknowledged this problem publicly when former Minister of Science and Technology General Vo Nguyen Giap wrote: "Another imperative is to abolish the bureaucratic system of management which has stunted the dynamism of economic and scientific activities [and] recognize the autonomy of individual establishments." The scientific community, however, is skeptical about the rate of progress. An official at one of Hanoi's most prestigious institutes told me: "Although the government pays lip service to science, it has yet to back it up with the kind of priorities and financial support needed. Until policies change, even though we have some brilliant scientists, Vietnam will continue to be outside the mainstream of world science and technology." Ill.121

The Economy

"We are not economists; we are revolutionaries. We were very good at war,
but management is much more difficult."

Nguyen Chi Chung, District Party Committee General Secretary

After seemingly endless years of sacrifice, independence did not bring the better life that the Vietnamese people had dreamed of. Hopes for a united, prosperous country dissolved in the face of post-war realities: isolation from Western trade and aid, natural catastrophes, and inept leadership.

In 1990, Vietnam's per capita annual income was about $120 while neighboring states ranged from $600 to $3,000. Consumer products are in extremely short supply, more than half of the children suffer from malnutrition, and the population rate is increasing by an estimated 1.2 million people every year. Unemployment has been nearly thirty percent, inflation rampant, and everyone has to work at two jobs to maintain even a minimal existence.

That Vietnam remains one of the poorest nations in the world is due in no small part to the United States embargo, vetoes on aid from international financial organizations, and American hindrance of private humanitarian efforts. British authorities in Hong Kong and spokesmen of other nations blame the United States for the continuing flow of refugees attempting to escape Vietnam's unbearable poverty.

Hanoi's leaders in 1975 did not anticipate the problems they would incur when they attempted to impose onto the South's free-wheeling economy the rigidly orthodox socialism that had been practiced in the North since 1954. In the power and economic vacuum created when the French left, implementing reforms in the North was relatively easy, perhaps because poverty there had long been extreme and people were willing to try anything new in hope of improvement. But the South for many years had enjoyed a higher standard of living generated by a viable capitalist economy, and in Saigon the post-1975 reforms sought by Hanoi found scant enthusiasm. The South's cooperation with Hanoi has been superficial at best.

With their backs to the wall, in 1987 high-level Party members admitted that drastic reforms were essential, and changes were announced in both domestic and foreign policy. Foreign Minister Nguyen Co Thach said, "There has not been enough spirit of democracy. We had government 'for the people,' when it must be 'of the people.' We had good intentions but bad means – which can destroy all good intentions."

Reforms included expanding the scope of the private sector, reducing the budget deficit, and boosting the output of agricultural and consumer goods for domestic use and exports. Results in some areas were rapid and dramatic; in less than a year, inflation declined to less than twenty-five percent, and there has been a certain amount of success in the area of foreign investment. But Vietnam's economy remains in dire straits.

Infrastructure

In Vietnam, a great many things just don't work. Decrepit and deteriorating highways, bridges, railways and rolling stock, telephone systems, water supply, waste disposal, power grids, oil pipelines, port facilities, and all the rest, are considered the most serious impediment to rapid improvement of the nation's economy. Foreign analysts attribute the crippling dysfunction to inadequate maintenance, insufficient spare parts, antiquated equipment and technology, and the "bloody-mindedness of many of the bureaucrats."

Transportation is inadequate, both internally and as a link to outside markets. In the cities, bicycles and motorcycles are the principal mode of transport for carrying goods and passengers; in the countryside they are augmented by people carrying goods on shoulder-poles. Small boats – rowed, poled, sculled, sailed, or driven by small motors – ply more than 4,000 miles of inland waterways. Roads are so bad that driving speeds average below twenty-five miles per hour. Damaged bridges frequently allow only one-way traffic, and traffic outside the cities is delayed by the many ferries in use where destroyed bridges have not been rebuilt.

Ill. 122-126

The national railway is a historic relic from the French Colonial era. One narrow-gauge track links North and South, and antiquated traffic controls limit the system to twelve pairs of trains. The locomotives, many of them steam relics more than sixty years old, average twenty miles per hour for passenger trains and thirteen for freight trains.

Air transport between Vietnam and the rest of the world has remained limited: until 1990, only three non-Communist airlines were permitted to fly into Hanoi and Saigon, although air service will certainly improve when international trade restrictions are lifted. In part because of their isolation, the Vietnamese had little idea of the generally high standards expected of modern airlines. Airport terminals are impossibly shabby, with almost no amenities. Vietnam's air traffic control (ATC) equipment is obsolete, unreliable, and considered dangerous by international standards.

In 1989 the national air carrier, Air Vietnam, operated twenty-six planes, almost all in poor condition, with seating capacity ranging from fourteen to 100. Demand for seats is so heavy that flights were routinely sold out months in advance, and because Air Vietnam does not belong to the International Air Transport Association (IATA) nor Vietnam to the International Civil Aviation Organization (ICAO), many safety regulations are ignored: baggage is crammed into the aisles, seat belts are missing or inoperable, seat backs flop back and forth, and passengers sometimes have to stand. Air Vietnam food is best not talked about, but is reportedly improving on the Bangkok run.

Vietnam's seaports have been unable to function to capacity since the war: warehouse space is woefully inadequate, the harbors are heavily silted. Because of maintenance problems, only about half of the fixed shore cranes are usable at any one time. Ships and fishing boats lie rusting for want of spare parts and paint. Many potentially useful inland waterways need dredging. Irrigation and flood control systems are almost entirely dependent on manual labor because there are few operable pumps in the country.

Electricity is unreliable, with chronic shortages throughout the country. The new Soviet-built power station at Hoa Binh, sixty miles south of Hanoi, is billed as the world's largest, but nearly twenty-five percent of its energy production vanishes in distribution and transmission losses. Subsidized rates charged for electricity do not begin to cover operating costs. Officials complain that it is difficult to bill customers accurately since many homes don't have meters – there aren't enough to go around – and many people simply tap into electrical street lines illegally. (A friend and I were dining in a second story private restaurant one evening, when it grew dark enough to need light; the owner casually climbed out the window and attached his electric wire onto the lines of a nearby electrical pole.)

My experience persuaded me that telecommunication in Vietnam would be better served by carrier pigeon. There are no pay phones, except those at the post office, for long distance only. Local calls are free, but locating a telephone and getting through is something else altogether. When (if) the connection is made, line static is frequent and severe. In 1989's statistics, the country is served by 0.16 telephones per 100 people (less than two in 1,000), virtually none of which are private, and no intercity dialing system is in place. The 1989 UNDP economic survey describes an immediate need for at least ten times the existing number of telephone traffic circuits. International phone service recently improved after an Australian company installed satellite communications equipment. During my Hanoi stay, the city's first public fax machine was installed as well.

Telegraph service is frequently unreliable. A Christmas message from my stateside family, for example, waited ten days in the post office, some twenty yards from where I lived. And I wouldn't have gotten it even then had I not been standing at the counter of the Thang Nhat Hotel when a messenger handed it to a clerk, asking if he had any idea to whom the telegram belonged. I just happened to be so close to it that I noticed my name at the top. Postal service, too, is expensive, slow, and erratic.

Agriculture

The government de-collectivized rice and food production beginning in 1987, with impressive results. By 1989, Vietnam exported 1.5 million tons of rice, to become the third-largest rice exporter in the world. This feat was accomplished using techniques that date back centuries, and throughout my stay in the country, I never saw any mechanized agricultural machinery. Simultaneously, the government is encouraging the cultivation of vegetables in an effort to improve the nutritional value of a diet that relies too much on rice.

Forestry accounts for approximately seven percent of Vietnam's gross national product. Roughly one-third of the nation's forests have been destroyed, mostly a result of U.S. bombing and defoliation, but also because there has been little replanting of trees used as firewood and timber. Lacking modern technology, the timber industry uses manual labor in practically all Ill. 127 stages of production. 129,131

Industry

Industrial growth and productivity has been impeded by shortages of spare parts, difficulties in importing supplies, insufficient energy, and the woeful transportation system. Heavy industry, concentrated in the North and employing only about one million people (out of sixty-seven million), includes iron and steel, chemicals, concrete, fertilizer, engines, vehicle parts, and agricultural implements. An estimated two million people work in cooperative and Ill. 128 private light industries, such as garment manufacture, bamboo and wooden furniture and 130, handicrafts, mostly located in Saigon. 132-133

The North has a rich supply of minerals, especially iron ore, bauxite, and tin, but few means to exploit them. However, Vietnam's large offshore oil reserves, being explored by dozens of oil companies, provide a ray of hope for the nation's economic troubles. American oil companies have not been able to secure leases or invest in oil refineries because of the U.S. embargo. Gleefully rubbing his hands together, one Canadian oilman told me, "All the small oil companies are delighted with Bush's embargo. If it weren't for that, none of us small oil companies could possibly compete here."

Tourism

Having witnessed the economic benefits tourism brought to its neighbors, Vietnam in 1987 began a campaign to attract Western visitors. The country's vast white sand beaches, turquoise seas, striking landscapes, historical sites, and other-worldly atmosphere are surely naturals for tourism. A French tour company organizes waterfowl safaris, and the government is preparing a program of big game hunting; rumor prices a bear at $3,000 and a tiger at $10,000. Wild animal reserves will be opened for photo excursions to observe Vietnam's estimated eighty species of animals, including elephants, wild buffalo, bears, tigers, panthers, and two hundred bird species.

Hanoi's hotel accommodations, devoid of charm and comfort, range from unacceptably primitive to basic, daunting even the hardiest travellers who routinely encounter exposed electrical wires, peeling paint, lumpy beds, nonfunctional plumbing, intermittent electricity, marginal lighting, and lots of scurrying little feet in unexpected places. Because of the North's isolation since 1954, hotels there are run by people who have never seen a Western hotel. While they had little trouble pleasing their Communist Bloc visitors, they have no knowledge of what the rest of the world expects in the way of facilities and service.

Even if Hanoi's hoteliers choose to raise standards, there is little they can change yet because the resources needed to make improvements are not available. Soap, wax, vacuum cleaners, and cleaning materials are rare commodities, when they can be had at all. The good news is that sheets and mosquito netting are clean, the floors mopped daily, and the personnel accommodating. Better news is that several of the lovely French Colonial hotels have been renovated, and new joint venture hotels have been built in both the North and South. New airplanes and Japanese tour vans have been ordered, and hotel managers are being sent to Bangkok for training.

One flashy exception to the bleak hotel scene glitters grandly in Saigon Harbor – an ultra-luxurious and exorbitantly priced floating hotel recently towed from Australia. Saigon has other acceptable hotels, left from American times.

But visitors agree that Vietnam's primary tourist attraction is the warmth and generous hospitality of its people. Completely reversing the reputation of most Communist countries, where service personnel were generally surly, arrogant, and utterly uninterested in their jobs, the Vietnamese (although not always sure what is expected) are anxious to please. Because, over the course of my stay in Hanoi I spent so much time in the lobby of the Thang Nhat Hotel (hoping to scrounge news magazines, newspapers, paperback books, or chocolate from foreign visitors, or information from journalists), I spoke with hundreds of tourists – as contrasted to aid workers or business people. Invariably I asked them if they would contemplate a return visit. Everyone but one French couple said "yes." My second question was, "What did you most enjoy about the country?" The answer was always, always, "The people."

Ill. 134, 137

Foreign Aid

Since 1975, Vietnam's economy has been dependent on foreign aid. The Soviet Union was the country's biggest benefactor but aid has been drastically reduced since the failure of Communism in Eastern Europe and the collapse of the former Soviet Union. United Nations agencies have helped, but in 1987 such assistance averaged only a little over two dollars per person, compared to fifteen dollars per person in Bangladesh, though Bangladesh has a higher per capita income than Vietnam.

Non-Communist countries such as Sweden, Germany, Finland, France, Italy, India, and Australia have also helped Vietnam with humanitarian and developmental aid. A few

American private groups with enough clout and moxie to overcome their government's obstacles, notably the Quakers and Mennonites, have been running successful humanitarian projects in both the North and South of Vietnam, during the war and after. Smaller groups have dedicated their energies and resources to helping the Vietnamese people, including many large and small war veterans' organizations, as well as overseas Vietnamese.

Foreign Trade

Foreign trade is being attracted by Vietnam's liberal financial code which permits up to 100% ownership for foreign capital investment. In early 1991, the leading foreign investors in Vietnam were from France, Canada, Great Britain, Belgium, and Japan. In Hanoi's hotels, blue-suited Japanese businessmen, grey-suited Germans, and casually-attired Thais are replacing the drably-clad Soviet and Eastern European bureaucrats.

I was surprised to meet American businessmen in Hanoi a few months after I'd arrived, and later encountered oil executives and technicians there to "scout the territory" in anticipation of an end to the United States embargo.

Foreign investors are interested in Vietnam's abundant natural resources which are to date under-utilized, including the enormous potential for the development of ocean and river fish and shellfish. The country's extensive coastline and navigable rivers also favor the development of trade.

Overseas Workers

Before journeying to Vietnam, I had read articles in American newspapers that told of Vietnam's government sending its unwilling citizens as virtual slave laborers to the Soviet Union. I found the facts exactly the opposite: the Vietnamese overseas workers' programs have significantly enriched Vietnam's economy, and overseas work has eased domestic unemployment. The Vietnamese government retains a portion of all salaries earned overseas, but even with a ten to forty percent "commission" going to the government, those working overseas earn and save much more than they could possibly have done in Vietnam. As a result, overseas jobs are highly prized and eagerly sought, even though such employment often meant four year tours abroad, with only one visit home (at the worker's expense). Overseas employment was also a privilege because of the Eastern European consumer items that could be brought back, and the opportunity to learn another language and new technical or managerial skills – important assets on the return home.

Since 1980 Vietnam has sent 220,000 workers abroad: 210,000 of them to Eastern Europe and the USSR, and 10,000 to Africa or the Middle East (Algeria, Iraq, and Libya). Because of the Gulf War and the political upheavals of Eastern Europe, however, this source of employment has dwindled to a trickle.

Remittances and Investment by Overseas Vietnamese

Vietnam's economy has been partially dependent on the approximately $200 million pumped into it by goods and funds sent home to relatives from overseas. An example is Kristy Tran, a nineteen-year-old college student living in the United States who works to send money to her mother. "Fifty dollars here can support my mother and brother for a month," she says. " I send them about $600 a year." Saigon authorities claim one-third of the city's population (more than one million) exist solely on foreign remittances and packages.

Hanoi encourages overseas Vietnamese (Viet Kieu) to return home to visit relatives and explore investment projects. In 1990, according to government figures, over 40,000 Viet Kieu returned home, 15,800 from the United States. A special department handles their travel plans and inquiries, and they are invited (but not obligated) to stay in special hotels offering accommodations as good as the tourist hotels, for a third of the price. During Tet the airports are thronged with overseas Vietnamese, easily identifiable in their Western clothes and designer sunglasses.

A few Viet Kieu have even returned to Vietnam on a permanent basis. One is Professor Nguyen Le Trang, who left Saigon in 1955 to study and work in Paris, where he remained until 1980. From 1980 to 1985 Dr. Trang worked as a successful medical researcher in New York City at Rockefeller University, then returned to Paris for two more years. In 1987 he chose to return to Vietnam and is now living in Hanoi, working at the Institute for Hygiene and Epidemiology. Dr. Trang showed me some American medical journals with articles about his work in the United States, and when I asked him why he gave up a prestigious position, a good salary, and luxurious living to return to the poverty of Vietnam, he answered, "Sometimes in life you must make the good choice."

Ill. 135

In describing his reception when he returned to Vietnam, Dr. Trang said, "At first my neighbors suspected me of being a CIA spy, since no one could imagine why I would give up living in the West to return to Hanoi." He claims the initial coldness did not bother him. "I felt good in my skin and did not care what they thought. I have interesting work to do, and my director has full confidence in me. Now people seem to accept me. My only sacrifice is that I don't have easy access to Western scientific journals, papers, and conferences. I don't even get sick from the food anymore!"

Conclusion: an American in Hanoi

The Vietnamese seem to feel a genuine affection toward Americans. Without exception, the dozens of American veterans groups I met in Hanoi told me they'd been amazed to encounter so much warmth from the people, as well as the government. There was the group of four vets who had just completed a tour of Vietnam and planned to confront officials in Hanoi with demands for information on their "lost buddies, who were listed as missing in action." This was a different type of veteran from the others I'd met, most of whom had returned to Vietnam to try to deal with demons haunting them about what they had done or seen during the war. I asked if they had encountered any problems, considering they were walking around in baseball caps with conspicuous American flag badges on the front of them. One said, "When we left home, we were told to expect hostility, especially in the North. But if there's a hostile Vietnamese in this country, we haven't met him. The only problem we've had with the hats is that everyone wants to buy them."

In any gathering with other Westerners where I was introduced to Vietnamese as an American, attention immediately focused on me. Huge smiles broke out; people touched my arm in welcome. More than once, European embassy officials from one of the embassies giving considerable aid to Vietnam exhibited pique at such exuberant affection for an American. "Why do they act like that when your country continues to try to destroy theirs?" I had no answer.

My guess is that part of the reason for the official and individual warmth towards Americans is that during the war Hanoi was very aware of the anti-war movement in the United States, although it is now conceded by Vietnamese historians that they overestimated its importance. However, believing that it would be the American people, rather than the military, that would end the war, Hanoi propagandists perpetuated the idea that the American people were basically good – and even sympathetic to the Vietnamese fight for independence and unity. It was the American leadership that was portrayed as evil.

Similarly, during some of my more frustrating and trying experiences dealing with the Vietnamese bureaucracy – and there were times when I wanted to get on the next plane out – I used to remind myself to separate the Vietnamese people from their government. I often did meet good people in the government. Many officials went out of their way to make my stay agreeable and make me feel appreciated even though, through a combination of ignorance, American impatience, or insatiable curiosity, I inadvertently trampled over Vietnamese custom and rules. The smiles, though at times strained, never ceased.

The government must, however, be given credit for the fact that it permitted an American to live in Vietnam at a time when the American government, continuing its intransigent and hostile rejection of Vietnam's pleas for normalizing diplomatic relations, confined Vietnamese in the United Nations delegation to an area within 25 miles of New York.

However, long after the political gestures are forgotten, it is the warmth of the people I'll treasure. The kindnesses extended to me each day are too numerous to list. A few I'll always remember are:

...the old woman who hunkered next to me on the sidewalk on a sweltering day and fanned my face while I sat on a small stool eating noodle soup. Unfortunately, I didn't speak enough of the language to find out anything about her, nor she about me. But the smiles and gestures counted for some sort of communication.

...the chambermaids and houseboy of the hotel who knocked on my door on Christmas morning to give me carefully wrapped Christmas presents I was sure they couldn't afford, and again at Tet.

...the anonymous woman who slipped an envelope under my apartment door the last Christmas I spent in Hanoi. Inside was a small, hand-crocheted doily, with a card that said, "This a present for Christmas. I made it." There was a signature, but I was unable to locate the person. I pinned a note of thanks to my door, but never discovered my benefactor.

...the street artist who, almost aggressively, insisted on drawing my portrait, taking a long time over it while I embarrassedly sat on a tiny three-legged stool on the sidewalk, in front of a growing crowd. When he presented me with a very good likeness, the crowd clapped with approval; when he refused to take any money, they clapped louder.

Ill. 136

...the small girl selling tea on a street corner I frequently passed on my bike, who refused my money for a cup of tea. (In return, I took her photograph and, to her huge delight, later gave her copies of it.)

...the countless people in the street who gladly posed for my camera, many of whom gathered their neighbors and children to make my pictures more interesting. As often as not, they would invite me to have tea with them.

...and the cyclo driver (whom I'd helped with his halting English), who pedalled more than six miles dressed up in a frayed dark Western suit, shirt, and tie, to deliver a wrapped bouquet of flowers to me on the morning I left Hanoi for the last time. He was not permitted to enter the compound where I lived and had to wait for me outside at the street entrance. After he gave me the flowers, I kissed him on both cheeks – to the smiles and applause of a dozen or so Vietnamese who'd stopped on the street to watch the small ceremony.

These and all the rest of the Vietnamese deserve better than what they now have. The Communist Party paper *Nhan Dan* promises, "The winds of change are in the air." These brave people have been patient; let's hope the winds will soon bring a better life to a nation that is long overdue for a bit of good fortune.